Bright
Candles

A Novel of the Danish Resistance

Bright Candles

A Novel of the Danish Resistance

by Nathaniel Benchley

Harper & Row, Publishers
New York, Evanston, San Francisco, London

BRIGHT CANDLES

The passage on page 151 is taken from *The Moon Is Down* by John Steinbeck, and is quoted with permission of Mrs. John Steinbeck and The Viking Press.

Library of Congress Catalog Card Number: 73-5477
Trade Standard Book Number: 06-020461-3
Harpercrest Standard Book Number: 06-020462-1

NOTE:

With obvious exceptions, the main characters in this book are fictitious; the main happenings are history. Once or twice I have had to invoke the novelist's privilege of warping time and juggling facts, but I hope these minor distortions will be evident only to Danes with long memories.

It is a curious fact that Danes who were involved in the resistance are reluctant to talk about their experiences, to the point where they become virtually mute. They have a terror of appearing to boast; they are embarrassed when they hear of one who may have talked, and they prefer to treat the whole experience as though it had been a trip to the office. This, as may well be imagined, makes it difficult for one not involved to ferret out any but the bare historical facts, and only with promises of anonymity are any personal experiences ever elicited. However, it would be no less than churlish of me if I were not to thank ***, whom I bludgeoned into agreeing to check this manuscript for errors, either of fact or of feeling, and whose contribution goes beyond any chance of being repaid.

—N.B.
Tivoli Gardens, May, 1973

***name deleted by request

Bright Candles

A Novel of the Danish Resistance

Chapter One

They say you can never go home again, and I suppose in a
sense that's true. I went back to Copenhagen recently, having
been away for what seemed like a lifetime, and while everything was outwardly the same—the same Town Hall clock
tower, the red tile roofs and broad streets and green copper
spires and turrets—there was still something missing. I don't
know what it was, but the feeling was different: There wasn't
the sense of excitement I'd known before. There were Germans around, but now they were tourists or businessmen, and
of course you could no longer harass them. That's probably
what I missed.

I'm sure that sounds odd and I probably shouldn't have
said it, because many of the Germans in Copenhagen now
weren't even born during the Occupation, but some things
take a long time to forget. What I'm trying to say is that it
was a time of danger and daring; we felt we were doing some-

thing worthwhile, and because we were young we looked at it almost as a game. And if *that* sounds odd I'm sorry. It's the way it was.

As long as I live, I will remember the morning of Tuesday, April 9, 1940. I was sixteen, and was looking forward to the next month, when my seventeenth birthday would coincide with the annual opening of the Tivoli Gardens, an amusement park in the center of Copenhagen. Tivoli isn't very big, but it has all the magic of Hans Andersen's stories. Rides, music, restaurants, dancing—it's a place where the old feel young again, and the young feel drunk with the joy of being alive. And to have your birthday happen on the opening of Tivoli is to have the best party anyone could imagine. I was hoping I could get Ingrid Nielsen to come with me, but hadn't yet got up the nerve to ask her.

This particular Tuesday started off like any other. My mother was up first, and while she was warming the sweet rolls and setting out the sausage and cheese for breakfast, my father shaved and I waited my turn in the bathroom, flicking through the schoolwork I had theoretically studied the night before. It was a beautiful day, bright and cold. Overhead came the sound of an airplane, and then another, but I didn't pay much attention because I'd suddenly come on a passage from Ovid I was supposed to have memorized and had somehow completely overlooked. I heard more airplanes, and for a moment was tempted to go to the window to look, but the terror of being called on to recite the unlearned passage outweighed everything else, and I frantically began to try to commit it to memory. (To this day I still haven't learned it, and by now I don't think I'm likely to.) Then I heard the sound of the radio, and the announcer's voice had a queer tone that made me stop and listen. I got up slowly and went to the kitchen, where my mother was staring at the radio as though it were a snake. Together we listened, and

I heard the announcer saying, ". . . early this morning. At six AM, King Christian X ordered an end to all resistance, and the Germans began a systematic and peaceful occupation of the country. The note, which Herr von Renthe-Fink handed to Foreign Minister Munch at four thirty AM today, stated that the occupation was to protect Denmark from British aggression, and that the German Government had no intention, either at present or in the future, of interfering with the territorial integrity or political independence of the Kingdom of Denmark. It is expected that the *Rigsdag* will go into emergency session as soon as . . ."

"They can't *do* that!" my mother shouted at the radio. "There was an agreement! Who do they think they are?" She was in her mid-thirties, and her round face and blonde hair still had some of the shine of youth, but when she was worked up, as she was now, her softness disappeared and she looked suddenly older.

I ran to the bathroom, and pounded on the door. "In a minute," came my father's voice. "A little patience, please."

"Papa!" I cried. "We've been invaded!" But the noise of the flushing toilet drowned out my voice, and all I could do was continue to beat on the door.

"Jens, I said in a minute!" my father said, more sternly. "Your turn will come."

"Papa!" I bellowed. "The Germans! They're here! Germans!"

There was a pause, then the key turned in the latch, and the door opened a crack. My father's thin face, streaked with the remains of his shaving lather, peered out at me. The top button of his underwear was undone, and his suspenders hung down around his haunches. "What are you talking about?" he asked.

"Just that! We've been invaded! It's on the radio!"

He stared at me for a moment. "Are you serious?"

3

"Yes!" Remembering the noise of the airplanes, I ran to the window and looked upward, where a formation of dragon-fly-like bombers was lazily circling the city. Every now and then, on the closer ones, you could see the black crosses on their wings. "Look up there!" I said, pointing.

My father followed me and peered at the planes, then began to slide his suspenders up over his shoulders. "Was there a battle?" he asked.

"I don't know. The man just said we gave up."

He headed back for the bathroom. "Probably just as well," he said. "The Poles tried to resist, and look what happened to them."

My mother had come into the room, and her blue eyes were shining with rage. "Ole Hansen!" she said. "Is that all you have to say? Your country is invaded, and you shrug it off as though it were a soccer match?"

He looked back at her quietly. "What would you like me to say?" he asked. "Do you want me to put my head out the window and tell them to go away?"

"But you needn't be so—so smug about it!"

"I'm nothing of the kind. I just don't see there's anything I can do."

"But they signed a non-aggression pact! Isn't that supposed to mean anything? And our Government said we'd resist if we were invaded! What happened to that? Don't the politicians mean *anything* they say?"

I should put in here that my father had a job in the accounting department of the newspaper *Politiken*, and this led people to believe he had an inside knowledge of what went on in the news. My mother's friends were always asking what her husband had heard about this or that, or what he felt might happen in such and such a case, and she had finally come to accept the myth herself, although in her heart she probably knew he didn't know any more than anyone else. I think

4

perhaps she hoped he did, and tried to make her hope a fact. She almost never argued with him, and this was the first time I'd ever heard her raise her voice to him. He didn't seem to be aware she was shouting; his voice was as calm as though he were buying a hat.

"They may mean it at the time," he said. "Some of them do, and some of them don't. But then situations can alter, and they have to take a new approach."

"Well, you're not going to make *me* like it."

"I didn't say I *liked* it; I just said there was nothing I could do. Now, if you'll excuse me, I'm going to finish my toilet." He went back into the bathroom, and my mother glared at the closing door and then returned to the radio in the kitchen. I could hear her talking to it as though it were a person.

Your mind does strange things at times like this, and as I tried to digest what had happened I stared at a candle, which had been burning brightly last night and now was a black twig in a blob of white wax. (In Denmark, we use candles as well as electricity at night, and it wasn't until I went abroad that I discovered everyone doesn't do the same.) As I looked at this guttered candle I wondered if it was an omen of some sort; if it meant the end of everything or the existence of hope in the ruins, and while I would have liked to draw a neat comparison I couldn't quite make it fit, and I finally gave up. My mind was in a turmoil anyway, because I'd never seen my parents so sharply divided on any issue. I didn't like to take sides, but I shared my mother's outrage and her feeling we'd been tricked, and while I could see my father's point about not wanting to be wiped out the way Poland was, I still felt we shouldn't have given up immediately. Especially since, not three months before, the Government had unanimously declared we'd fight if we were invaded. It made a mockery of our Government, and therefore of us. And at sixteen you have enough worries, without being an object of derision to the entire world.

There was no conversation at breakfast; we were all listening to the radio. The only other news at that time was that Norway had also been invaded, and, to make the Danish position more humiliating, Norway was putting up a fight. My parents glanced at one another when this news was read, and although they didn't say anything the look in their eyes was eloquent. My mother's gleamed with a strange kind of triumph, while my father's tried to show indifference. He looked down almost immediately, and concentrated on his sausage. It seemed impossible that Norway could hold out without British help, but at least they were fighting.

It might be a good idea to explain that this was the end of the so-called *Sitzkrieg*, or "phony war." Germany had invaded Poland the previous September, and Britain and France, honoring their treaty commitments to Poland, declared war on Germany. Then Russia had jumped in, and before England and France could say "Boo" she and Germany had divided Poland between them, and the fighting was over. For the entire winter nobody fired a gun, and when spring came people began to wonder if everyone had forgotten there was supposed to be a war on. What happened to Norway and us in April was the beginning of the heat-up into the real thing.

When breakfast was over, my father wiped his mouth, rolled his napkin, and stood up. "You ready, Jens?" he said. He and I used to leave the house together, he to walk or take the tram to work, and I to ride my bike to school.

"Ready for what?" my mother asked. "Where do you think you're going?"

"To work," he replied. "This isn't a public holiday. As far as the paper is concerned, it's like any other day." As an afterthought, he added, "Perhaps with a little more news than usual." (My father was, generally speaking, a serious man, but every now and then he couldn't resist a small and understated joke.)

"We're as good as at war," my mother announced, "and you say it's like any other day! Did you see those bombers in the sky? Did you hear them threaten to blow us up? If you didn't, I did—it was on the news!"

"We are not at war," he said, patiently. "Those bombers were only in case we resisted. The Germans have said they'll respect our rights, and I assume they will."

"Do you think there'll be *school* on a day like today?" She was talking as though he'd suddenly started speaking Croatian.

"Until we know to the contrary, I do," he replied. "The main thing is not to panic. If we let the Germans interrupt our daily routine, we are lost. Come on, Jens, it's getting late."

Our house was on a small street off the Sortedams Sø, a stretch of water that was once part of the moat that surrounded the city. The city has long since leapfrogged the moat and grown outward, but the water remains, and it makes good skating when there's a hard freeze. The minute my father and I got to the street we felt something amiss, and it took us a moment to realize what it was: It was silence. Aside from the droning of the planes, there was no other sound—no traffic noises, no horns, no anything. We went up to Øster Søgade, the boulevard that runs along the water, and at the bridges that crossed it we saw long lines of people, standing. There wasn't a car in sight; just the distant people, and then, facing them, we saw a line of helmeted troops in gray uniforms. Nobody seemed to be moving, or doing anything in particular; the soldiers and the people were just standing there. The sun was bright but the air was cold, and my father flicked up the collar of his topcoat and turned away from the water. His office was just off Town Hall Square, and this is where we headed, he walking and I riding slowly beside him. For a while he didn't seem to notice me, and then, almost casually, he spoke.

"Aren't you going to school?" he asked.

"Papa, I'm sure there's no school today," I replied. "Nobody's going anywhere."

"You might try."

"How? You saw the troops across Øster Søgade."

"There's probably another way." He said it just because he felt he had to; I don't think he really believed it.

"Well, I'll try," I said, unconvincingly. "But I'm bound to be late, so I might as well be a little later. I'd like to see what's happening in Town Hall Square." He said nothing, and we went the rest of the way in silence.

Town Hall Square is so large that pedestrians can't cross it on one set of traffic lights; they have to make their way, light by light, to the center sections and then to the other side, as though crossing a desert from one oasis to another. The Town Hall, with its high, crenellated walls and green-spired Gothic clock tower, dominates one whole side of the Square, while hotels, restaurants, and office buildings enclose the rest. News kiosks and hot-dog stands and flower stalls are sprinkled throughout the center area, and pigeons and sparrows scuttle underfoot. Directly in front of the Town Hall is a forest of flagpoles, and when all flags are flying in a brisk wind they sound like a cavalry charge. When we reached the Square that morning, the silence was almost total. The center section was deserted, and long columns of people filled the sidewalks, facing the soldiers who lined the streets. The soldiers were impassive, holding their bayonets loosely pointed at the crowd, and seeing them close up I marveled at the amount of equipment they carried. They all wore the heavy boots, and the coal-scuttle steel helmets with small German eagles on either side, and in addition they were festooned with pouches and knapsacks and canisters and shovels and grenades, until some of them were almost pear-shaped. How they managed to get here so fast, and with all that equipment, was a complete mystery. (As it turned out, these had come off an innocent-looking German merchant ship, which had docked unchallenged at Langelinie, near the Little Mermaid statue.)

My father and I stood, with the other silent Danes, looking at the soldiers, and the soldiers looked back at us as though we were cattle. It crossed my mind that these troops might very well have been among those who had laid waste to Poland in such short order, and it seemed impossible that anything could stand against them. Then I saw one of them look at the man next to him, wet his lips, and smile, and I thought, What do you know? They're human, after all. It made me feel better for a minute, but then the shame of our having given in came back worse than before, and I felt terrible.

"I can't stand here all day," my father said, abruptly turning away. "I have work to do. Jens, I suggest you go home." I said nothing, and my father disappeared into the crowd.

Then an odd thing happened. There came the frantic beeping of a horn, and a purple delivery truck from Illums Department Store forced its way into the Square, scattering people right and left. We all stared in disbelief, wondering if the driver had gone berserk and was trying to run down the Germans single-handedly, but then it pulled up to a corner and stopped, and two German soldiers got out. They opened the back and began to unload coils of barbed wire. They were joined in a couple of minutes by a truck from the Magasin du Nord with a similar cargo, and then the whole thing became clear : The Germans had commandeered whatever transportation they could find until their own rolling stock should arrive. At my elbow, a voice said, "I hope the swine drop it in their laps," and I turned and saw my friend Ole Suensen. His face was grim.

"A fine thing, isn't it?" I said.

"I think I'll volunteer," said Ole.

"For what?"

"To fight in Norway. At least they've got some guts."

"How's it going there?"

"I don't know. I hear the English have landed."

"That would be good."

"Anything would be good except standing around with our thumbs up our behinds." Ole had red hair, which usually made him look slightly comical, but today his rage and despair made him look sick.

"Do you have any ideas?" I asked.

Ole reached in his pocket, and produced a piece of paper. "Have you seen this?"

"No." I took it. "Where'd you get it?"

"They dropped them from the planes. They're all over the place."

I read the paper, which was a bulletin to the Danish troops and the Danish people, explaining in a clumsy mixture of Danish, Norwegian, and German the reasons for the "protective action." It blamed the English and French for the war, and blathered on about how Churchill had designs on the freedom of the Scandinavian countries, and how the gentle Germans were going to protect us from the evils of war. I handed it back.

"So?" I said.

"So I don't know," Ole replied, stuffing the paper in his pocket. "But if they think we'll be taken in by crap like that, then maybe we could put out some bulletins of our own, and give them something to think about."

"Like what?" I was beginning to be interested.

"I said I don't know. All I know is if they're this stupid, there's got to be something we can do."

"You name it, and I'll do it." For some reason, Ole and I

struck sparks when we were together; one of us would have an idea, which would lead the other into a better idea, and pretty soon we'd be off on some tangent which, often as not, led us into trouble. But it was fun in the doing. "How's your German?" I asked.

"Screw German," said Ole. "Make them translate it."

For the first time that day, I laughed. "We could pretend it's secret orders to a group of saboteurs, telling how to blow up the German headquarters. It would drive them crazy."

Ole considered this. "I have a better idea," he said at last. "Let's just go ahead and *blow* up the German headquarters."

I looked at him, to see if he was serious. "How?"

"Any number of ways."

My stomach turned faintly cold. "Maybe we should start on something a little simpler," I said. "I like the bulletin idea."

"So do I," said Ole. "I also like to look ahead."

I studied the German soldier nearest us, trying to think of something that might make him uneasy, or frightened, but nothing came. The flat, unsmiling face, the glinting bayonet, and the polished boots all seemed impervious to thought, let alone fear. There is, as I later found out, no real fear unless you think about it; there is sudden terror, but that is more easily controlled than the kind of fear that gnaws away over a period of time. The first thing we had to do was make these people think. I use the word "people" loosely, because except for the one I saw briefly smiling, they were as impersonal as tanks.

Ole had been studying the same soldier, and after a while he said, "You know what? The son of a bitch likes it."

"Likes what?" I asked.

"The attention. He's never had so many people looking at him. He's probably some dull Bavarian clot, who joined the army because his mother's a rotten cook."

I thought about this for a moment. "What does that do for us?"

Ole smiled. "Wouldn't it be wonderful if we all turned our backs on him? If everyone in the Square looked away and pretended he didn't exist, we'd take away the biggest thrill of his life. He'd be crushed."

"I wish we could do it," I said. "With all these people, it's not likely."

"No, but we can look through the bastards any time we pass them. Just make like they're a tree or a hydrant, and see what it does for their confidence. As a matter of fact—" He turned, and started away "—I don't know what we're doing giving him our time right now. There must be something better we can do."

As I followed him through the crowd I saw the tall, rangy figure of Holger Andersen, watching the soldiers. Holger was two years older than we were, and had been our patrol leader in the Boy Scouts before Ole and I had been separated from the organization for putting *snaps* in the Scoutmaster's canteen. (It was an all-day hike, and he barely made it home.) The main thing we remembered about Holger was that his mother used to make cookies and pastries for him to take along on the hikes. They tasted a good deal better than the food we cooked for ourselves. Holger saw me looking at him, and he waved and smiled.

"Hi, there!" he called, and started toward us.

"Hi," said Ole, wondering what was coming next. We hadn't seen much of Holger since we left the Scouts, and we didn't know what to expect.

"Quite a day, isn't it?" said Holger.

"In what way?" Ole replied, without expression.

"Well, it's not every day we get invaded, is it?"

"You sound as though you liked it," said Ole.

"Don't be silly, man," said Holger. "Nobody likes to have his country taken over."

"Then what are you smiling about?"

"Is there some rule against smiling? It's good to see you guys—I haven't seen you in a long time." There was a pause while he waited for a reply, but none came so he went on. "What have you been doing with yourselves?"

"This and that," said Ole.

"Been putting any more snaps in people's canteens?" Holger asked, laughing.

"No," said Ole. "The second time would be redundant. We believe in being original."

"Speaking of canteens—" Holger tilted his head toward the Germans—"did you see all the equipment those fellows carry?"

"We saw," said Ole. "What of it?"

"Nothing. But it's impressive—each one is a self-contained unit on his own."

"As opposed to what?" Ole was making Holger sweat for every point.

"As opposed to—well, the Scouts. There one man would have one job, another man another job, and so on, but these guys can each one do everything that's required. It's just efficient, that's all."

"I guess the Poles think so," said Ole.

Holger laughed. "You can say that again."

"If you love the Germans so much, why don't you join them?" Ole said.

"Damn it, Suensen, you're getting me all wrong," said Holger. "I'm as good a Dane as anybody—I love my country as much or more than you do. Just because I happen to admire efficiency, does that mean I'm in love with the Germans?"

"No," said Ole. "But it's the way to bet."

Holger's face darkened, and he moved toward Ole. "Are you calling me disloyal?"

Ole paused, then said, "Not a bit. Just speculating."

"Well, you can speculate about something else." Holger turned and stamped off into the crowd, and Ole and I looked at each other.

"Do you think I offended him?" Ole asked, with a faint smile.

"Not in the least," I replied. "He just remembered his mother had left a cake in the oven."

Ole laughed. "I almost told him the pigs on my grandfather's farm were loyal, too. But then I figured that would start a fight, and I didn't want the Germans to see Danes fighting each other."

There is a street that goes from Town Hall Square to a smaller square called Kongens Nytorv, winding like a footpath and changing its name four times in the process. Collectively it is known as Strøget, or Strolling Street. (It pronounces "struyet," which sounds a little like "street" if you say it fast enough.) Ole and I made our way to Strøget, which was crowded with angry, bewildered people. Some were angrier than others; some were in tears, and some were resigned, and every now and then there was a little knot of people, arguing. Generally speaking, Danes are cheerful, and polite, but this morning feelings were running so high that some of the niceties of polite dialogue were omitted.

"What do you mean, it's just as well?" I heard one man say. "Just as well for whom?"

"Just as well for us, you cheesehead," was the reply. "What would you have us do—throw bricks at them?"

"What do we have an army for?"

"For Christ's sake, the Army can't do anything if they're not up to strength! Munch didn't want to provoke the Germans!"

"And look what it got us! Because Munch is a pee-faced pacifist, we're all in the soup! It's disgusting, it's disgraceful, and it makes me ashamed to be a Dane!"

"At least you're a live Dane—look at it that way."

"A lot of good that does, if I've got to kneel down and kiss the Germans' big fat—"

"Hey, look!" somebody else said. "Look who's coming!"

Everyone looked where he pointed and saw, ambling down Strøget, a lone Danish soldier. He was unarmed, and was wearing a fatigue cap, and he appeared to be about nineteen. His uniform was too big in the collar, making his neck look thin and scrawny. He walked with the dazed expression of one just awakened from a deep sleep.

"Well, if it isn't our big, brave defender!" someone said. "How are things at the war, soldier?"

"Did they give you any medals?" someone else asked. "What kind of medal do you get for hiding under the bed?"

The soldier's eyes flicked toward the speakers and he slowed his pace, but he said nothing.

"If you're looking for Germans I know where you can find some," another man said. "Or are you pretending such people don't exist?"

A woman darted out of the crowd, screamed, "Coward! Traitor!" then reared back and blew a spray of spittle on the soldier's uniform. She scurried away, and his eyes were as wide as though she'd shot him.

"Hey, lady, cut it out," he said, wiping his jacket and face. "I don't give the orders."

"You ought to be ashamed of yourself!" she shrieked.

Then some men closed in around him, and the shouting became general and unintelligible. The man who had been defending the Army tried to pull them away and get to the soldier to protect him, but the people had found someone on whom to vent their frustration, and it was like trying to stop a swarm of bees. They didn't strike the soldier, or do him any harm, but in their rage they made it almost impossible for him to stand. The last I saw of him he was backed against a building, one elbow raised to shield his face, shaking his head in mute reply to the insults. I looked at Ole.

"You didn't want the Germans to see Danes fighting each other," I said.

"It might do them good to see this," he replied. "But me, I'd rather not watch. Come on."

When I got home, my mother was in a state of wild excitement. "Have you heard?" she said, as I came in the door. "The British have landed in Norway, and are driving the Germans into the sea!"

"Someone said they'd landed," I replied. "I didn't hear the rest."

"Mrs. Jørgensen heard it from a friend at the railroad station," she said, as though that clinched it. "They've sunk the *Bismarck*, and are chasing the *Tirpitz* to the north."

"Sounds as though they're having quite a day," I said.

"It just goes to show what can happen if you resist," my mother went on. "And I'm happy to say we didn't *all* give in like frightened rabbits. Prince Valdeman killed a German with his sword, right here on the streets of Copenhagen."

"Oh?" I said. "Then what happened?" Prince Valdeman, the Count of Rosenborg, was a relative of the King's and could expect a certain amount of immunity, but probably not for this.

"He's in hiding," she said. "They'll never find him."

"Where did this come from?"

"Mrs. Jakoby heard it. Mrs. Jakoby is in a state of absolute terror because she's afraid the Germans are going to come for her, and Mr. Jakoby is trying to remind her that Jews are different in Denmark, but she won't listen. She says Germans are the same everywhere, and he says they'd never dare do anything here, and there they are. Neither one can convince the other, and Mrs. Jakoby is about to jump out the window."

I thought of the German soldiers I'd just seen, and wondered if there was anything they wouldn't dare do, and it didn't take much thought to conclude they'd do exactly as they were told. It was up to their superiors what they did about the Jews, but none of us had ever thought of the Jews as being anything but Danes, so it was hard for us to make the distinction in our minds. It would have made as much sense for them to come for everyone who was left-handed, or who sang bass, or liked pomegranates. I couldn't think in their terms, so I decided not to try.

"Well, anyway, the Jakobys are safe," I said. "They've been here for three generations."

"That's what I told her," my mother replied. "But she's beyond listening to reason."

Later in the day the Government issued a proclamation, laying down the rules that were to govern our lives. There was a lot of verbiage, but what it all boiled down to was that if we cooperated with the Germans, they would give us as much independence in our domestic affairs as possible. In return for protecting us against the British, they would decide what was good for us and what wasn't. And our factories and farms would turn out materials for them as they were needed. The King added a personal appeal to the proclamation, asking us all to show correct and dignified conduct, because any rash actions or utterances would lead only to trouble. It was for our own good that he said it, and I suppose he had a point. At any rate, he was the one person who could have asked it of us.

"Well, there it is," my mother said, when the broadcast was over. "We have now become a nation of slaves."

I thought of Ole's and my plans for harassment, and decided it was better not to say anything. They sounded kind of childish, somehow, in the face of everything else.

When my father got home, she started asking him about

the British victories in Norway, and he sank into a chair and shook his head.

"Rumors," he said wearily. "Nothing but rumors. Not a word of truth in them."

"Did you hear about Prince Valdeman?"

"Another rumor. Untrue."

My mother's face fell. "Then what did happen?"

He smiled thinly. "You know as well as I do. We've been occupied." He thought for a moment, then laughed. "There was one interesting thing," he said. "There's a new man on the assignment desk, and when he heard the Germans were landing at the airport he sent a reporter out to interview them. You can imagine how much of a story *that* boy got."

My mother stared at him. "And that's our news for today?"

"That's about it," my father said. "It's all I can think of right now." He looked out the window at the gathering darkness, and added, "Oh, yes, We'll have to put up blackout curtains. No lights can show in the windows at night."

And that was the way the night came to us, a night that was to last for five long years.

Chapter Two

The first news of what really happened that day arrived in a strange manner. On Saturday morning, when the postman brought the mail, my father found in it a light blue envelope, addressed to him with no other name or return address on it.

"I wonder what this can be," he said, glancing at the back, and then at the handwriting.

"Why not open it and find out?" my mother suggested. "It looks as though it's from a woman."

"Don't be silly," my father replied. "I don't know any women."

"Thank you very much," my mother said.

"You know what I mean," he muttered, still staring at the writing.

"Open the letter!" my mother commanded. "I'm dying of curiosity!"

He took his butter knife, wiped it on his napkin, then very carefully slit the back of the envelope and extracted the letter. I think he was trying to tease her, because he unfolded the letter with deliberate care, cleared his throat, then took off his glasses and polished them. Then he read the letter, and his expression changed, and he was silent.

"What does it *say?*" my mother cried.

He read it through, then said, "It's an account of the battle last Tuesday."

"What battle? Where?"

"Apparently there was a fight at the border, when the Germans crossed into Jutland. Our troops resisted, and—and thirteen were killed. They also killed some Germans, and wounded a number."

"Who says so?"

He handed the letter across to her, and I read it over her shoulder. It didn't give the source; it just said that this was what had really happened, and it asked that we make ten copies of the letter and send them to people we thought might be interested in the truth. I should explain that the Germans had taken charge of the Danish press and radio, and since they wanted to make it look as though we'd welcomed them as protectors, not a hint of opposition was allowed. Their declared intention was to make themselves systematically loved (*"Wir werden uns systematisch beliebt machen"* was the way they put it), and they tried to maintain this fiction in the face of mounting opposition. It almost made you feel sorry for them.

"That's going to be a kind of risky thing," my father said.

My mother looked up from the letter. "What is?"

"Making all those copies. Suppose we get caught."

"Who's to catch us?"

He tried to think of an answer but couldn't, and his hands floundered about in the air. "I guess what I'm trying to say is it's against the King's directive," he said, at last. "It's against the spirit of it, anyway."

"To spread the truth?" Her voice held a tinge of contempt.

"Well, in the first place we don't know it's the truth. In the second place . . ." Again he looked for words, and again he was lost.

"In the second place?" she prompted him.

"I don't know. If we're going to have to live with these people we're going to have to live with them, and I don't see the point in doing something that's deliberately designed to rile them up."

"It's no such thing. It's the simple dissemination of the truth."

"And as I said, we don't know it's the truth."

"What do you think? What's your guess?" She was acting like a prosecutor with a reluctant witness. "Do you think it's the truth, or don't you?"

He looked across at the letter, which she was holding, and after a few moments he said, "Yes. I guess it probably is."

"Then do you have any objection to your countrymen knowing the truth?"

"No."

"Then what are we arguing about?"

"Nothing, I guess."

"All right, let's get started. Jens, fetch me some writing paper, will you?"

"I have a better idea," I said. "There's a mimeograph machine at school, and I can slip in there after hours and knock off a hundred copies."

My father looked as though I'd squirted boiling water in his ear. "You'll do no such thing!" he shouted. "You'll keep that letter here until the copies are posted, and then you'll destroy it!"

Of course, by the time I'd helped make the ten copies I

knew the letter by heart. I volunteered to take the copies down to the mailbox, and my father looked at me thoughtfully before he spoke.

"Come right back here when you've posted them," he said.

"I can't," I replied. "I've got a date with Ole Suensen."

"To do what?"

"I don't know what we're going to *do*. I just said I'd meet him today."

He continued to look at me. "See you don't get in any trouble."

"Yes, sir."

"All right. Be careful."

"Of what?"

"You have illegal literature there. Don't let anyone catch you."

"No, sir. I won't."

I went out, and as I walked to the mailbox I had the feeling I was carrying a bomb in my pocket. I put on a great show of carefree whistling, but all the time I was looking out of the corner of my eye for Germans, and wondering what I'd do if one should stop me and search me. I'd read of spies eating their messages, but the idea of wolfing down ten sealed and stamped letters was less than appealing, and I didn't know how I'd divert the German's attention while I was doing it. My mind took off, as it did when I was clowning with Ole, and I heard myself saying to the German, "Excuse me, sir, you don't by any chance have some mustard on you, do you?" Then, when he was searching his pockets for the mustard, I'd gobble the— The insanity of my daydream overcame me, and I began to laugh. I was still laughing as I slipped the letters in the mailbox, and I slammed the slot cover closed and turned around and found myself staring into the eyes of a German soldier. He'd been on the opposite corner as I approached, and I'd been so intent on the letters I hadn't seen him. The laugh faded from my face, and I felt my throat close. He looked at me for what seemed like a full minute, and then he spoke.

"*Warum lachst du?*" he said.

I had enough German to know he was asking why I was laughing, but I wasn't going to let him know that. So I pretended to misunderstand, and in Danish I said, "It's three blocks down on the right. You can't miss it." I pointed behind him, hoping he didn't see how violently my hand was shaking.

"*Bitte?*" he said.

"There's a big sign on it," I said, as though I were talking to a child. "There's even a light on it at night."

"*Versteh' nicht,*" he said.

I felt I couldn't keep this up indefinitely, so, speaking as bad German as I could, I said, "*Sie wollen das Herrenpissenplatz, nicht?*"

I thought he was going to fall over. He began to laugh, shaking his head and saying, "*Nein . . . nein . . .*" but he couldn't say any more, so I began to laugh with him. We stood there and chortled like a pair of idiots, and finally, in Danish, I said, " *That's* what I was laughing at," and walked away. I wondered if he was going to go looking for the men's room where I'd pointed, and decided it didn't matter. These people aren't so tough, I told myself. They're as easy to fool as children.

I met Ole at the Nytorv, or New Market, a square halfway along Strøget. I told him of my encounter with the German, and he enjoyed the joke, and then I asked him if his family had received a letter like ours.

"No," he said. "I've heard of them, but we haven't got one yet."

"Well, you will tomorrow," I told him. "I just posted it. In case you can't wait, here's what it says." I recited the letter to him, and his eyes grew wide with excitement.

"Hey!" he said. "Isn't that something!"

I thought of my idea of mimeographing it, and of my father's reaction, and as I examined his words in retrospect I thought I saw a loophole. He had said I would keep the letter in the house until the copies were posted, and then destroy it. In other words, he had forbidden me to take the letter to school to be mimeographed, but he had said nothing about my taking it in my head. The letter had been destroyed and the copies posted, so there was no evidence, and I felt I could make a case for having obeyed my part of the injunction. Not a very good case, perhaps, but an arguable one.

"I have an idea," I said to Ole. "It's going to take these chain letters a little while to get all over town. Suppose we were to borrow the school's mimeograph machine to bang out a few hundred extra copies, and kind of leave them around. How would that sound to you?"

Ole pursed his lips, and looked at the sky. "Beautiful," he said. "We could get on top of some building and let them drift off with the wind, and nobody'd ever know where they came from."

"Or fold them into paper airplanes," I suggested. "That way, they'd travel farther."

"Oh, my, yes," said Ole. "I see a full-blown project here."

"The first problem is to get the machine," I said. "They probably keep the office locked on the weekends."

"Don't let that worry you for an instant," said Ole. "I have an uncle who's a locksmith."

"So what do we do first?"

"I'd say we call on my uncle."

We started down Strøget, excited by the idea of our project, and Ole said, "What do the letters DKS mean to you?"

I thought for a moment, then said, "Nothing. Why?"

"Remember the idea I had, about looking at Germans and pretending they're not there?"

"Yes." I thought of the German I'd met at the mailbox,

and wondered how I could have pretended he didn't exist.

"Well, some other people have had the same idea. They've formed the DKS, or Danish Cold Shoulder Society, and they make out there isn't a German within miles. They've even put out little lapel buttons."

"How is it working?"

"It's too early to tell. Things like that take a while to sink in."

Thinking of the initials, I said, "I saw some letters on the side of Town Hall yesterday. SSU. Do you know what that means?"

Ole smiled. "*Smid Svinene Ud*—drive the swine out."

"How do you know?"

"I put them there. And I'm going to put them on the d'Angleterre as we go by." The Hotel d'Angleterre, a large, gleaming white luxury hotel on the Kongens Nytorv, had been taken over by the German Army brass. Their organizational setup was such that they eventually needed three headquarters: the d'Angleterre for the staff and high Army muckamucks; Shell House for the Gestapo, or secret police; and Dagmar House for the Nazi Party functionaries. Dagmar House, a dull gray office building on Town Hall Square, had SS elite guards in chest-high sentry boxes, while the d'Angleterre was guarded by Army personnel. Parenthetically, the professional Army officers scorned the Nazis and despised the Gestapo, who were scum sucked up from the gutters.

From the distance ahead there came the sudden sound of music, and we looked at each other in wonder. No Danish band would be playing so this must be German, and the prominent sound of the tuba confirmed this. They were beating out a rousing martial air, and the music came echoing down Strøget from the Kongens Nytorv. Kongens Nytorv (King's New Market) is a square with a planted area in

25

the center, and the trees and bushes and flowers make it more like a small park than anything else. The Germans had set up their band in the center part, and were oompahing away loud enough to wake the dead. When we got close enough I could see the conductor, flailing the air with his arms until I thought his suspenders would break, and the back of the tuba player's neck was red and distended. They were playing what they thought was cheerful music, and they were damned well going to see to it that the Danes enjoyed it. ("Wir werden uns systematisch beliebt machen.") The only trouble was that the Danes wouldn't listen. They walked through the square as though the musicians were so many pigeons, and the only person I saw who even acknowledged their presence was one man who, without breaking stride, fished in his pocket and brought out a coin, and tossed it at them. I would like to say it hit the conductor on the back of the head, but it didn't. It vanished, but the gesture remained.

We looked toward the d'Angleterre, and saw that it was bustling with activity. Army staff cars and black Mercedes sedans were drawn up in front, and a constant stream of porters and enlisted men was unloading baggage from a lorry. Two sentries flanked the entrance, presenting arms when the officers came through and looking stonily at everyone else. Ole studied the scene in silence for a few moments.

"And that's where you're going to put your SSU?" I said.

"Maybe," he replied. "I'm working on a better idea."

"Like what?"

"If we were to pretend we were workmen carrying something, we could get into that place like nothing at all."

"Hey, come on, Ole," I said. "Cut it out."

"I'm serious. Those guards pay attention only to the officers."

"What would we do once we were in there?"

"That would depend."

Ole had the knack of thinking of ideas so outrageous that his previous ones seemed tame by comparison. "Let's just settle for writing on the wall," I said. "Let's not try to do everything at once. Next you'll want to go to Berlin and kidnap Hitler."

"It would be a neat trick, if we could do it," he replied. "Come on."

As we approached the hotel, he motioned me to walk ahead of him. I did, and could feel my heart begin to beat faster. "Closer!" Ole hissed, behind me. "Get closer!"

"We're getting there," I replied, not turning around. "Do you want me to run?"

"Closer to the wall, you flathead! My arms aren't barge poles!"

I realized I'd been walking almost on the curb, subconsciously ready to dart across the street, so I edged closer to the side of the hotel, trying to look as though undecided as to whether or not to lean against it. I feigned interest in the band, then pretended I'd seen something fascinating in the stonework on the hotel wall, and I was just about out of subterfuges when I heard Ole say, "OK. Let's go."

"Where?" I asked.

He appeared beside me. "Just keep walking. God, you'd make a rotten saboteur. You'd be caught within an hour."

"I hadn't been thinking of sabotage," I replied.

"Well, you'd better start. It's going to be all the rage around here."

We passed the entrance to the hotel, threading our way through the baggage carriers, and nobody paid us any attention. We turned down the next side street, and I began to breathe more easily.

"You see?" Ole said. "If we'd been carrying something, we could have gone right in."

"Oh sure," I replied. "And most likely stayed in, too."

"Don't be defeatist," said Ole. "Hey, look." He pointed to a small, black car, parked at the curb. It looked like a large ladybug, and for a moment it was hard to tell which way it was headed. "That must be one of those Volkswagens," he said. "Hitler was going to make them for the German people, until he got the idea that war would be more fun."

"I don't see any officers riding around in that," I observed. "It must be for enlisted men."

"Enlisted men don't have cars of their own," said Ole. "It must be for lesser Party poops. I wonder how it works." He went to the front, took the handle on the hood, and tugged at it. It was locked. "By damn," he said. "They lock their engines." He circled the car, and saw another handle at the rear. "If they lock the engine they must lock the luggage—" He turned the handle, and there was the engine, looking not much bigger than a pencil sharpener. "Well, what do you know?" said Ole. "What won't these people think of next?" He squatted down. "But I'll bet they have distributors, just like other cars, and if they have distributors then all we need is to pull one little wire—"

I was suddenly aware of someone beside me, and I looked around and saw a tall, lean man in the black uniform of the SS. On his collar were the two lightning jags of the elite corps, and his face was hard and wolflike. "Ole!" I shrieked, and Ole straightened up so fast he almost fell over.

"What do you think you're doing?" the SS man said, in heavily accented Danish.

Ole swallowed, put one hand on the car to steady himself, and said, "You're just the person I was looking for. Can you explain to me how this works?"

"Take your hands off that car!" the SS man snapped, and out of some distant reflex Ole came to attention.

"I was admiring the workmanship," he said, trying to keep his voice steady. "German workmanship, as we know, the best in the—"

"What does it mean?" the SS man demanded.

Ole's eyes clouded. "What does that mean? I said German workmanship—"

"What do the letters mean?"

"The—?" Slowly, and with horror, Ole was beginning to understand.

"SSU. That you scrawled on the wall."

"Oh, that." Ole swallowed again, and tried to smile. "That means 'Up the SS.' It's a—well, you know—sort of a compliment."

"You lie."

"No, sir." Ole's voice rang with sincerity. "I wouldn't lie about a thing like that. I think the SS are just great. If they accepted Danes, I'd join it in a flash. The cream of the cream, they are."

The SS man's face remained stony. "You will come with me, and you will erase what you wrote on the wall." His eyes flicked toward me. "You, too." He drew himself up, heels together and shoulders squared. "March!"

We marched.

Around in front of the hotel, feeling as though we were naked in front of the world, we faced the letters that Ole had scrawled in charcoal pencil. We didn't know what to do, because the charcoal had worked into the pores of the stone, and when we rubbed it with our handkerchiefs it simply smudged.

"It won't come off," Ole said, at last.

"Keep working," said the SS man.

We kept working, but it only made the smudges worse, and finally the SS man realized that this could go on all day. "You," he said to me, and I turned and faced him, wondering if I was going to be shot. "Go into the hotel kitchen, and get a cleaning powder."

I started to obey, then said, "Will they give it to me?"

"Tell them *Standartenführer* Schlemmer has ordered it."

"Yes, sir." I zipped into the hotel, through the crowded lobby, and back to the kitchen, where I explained to a harried busboy what I wanted. He gave it to me and I returned, feeling as though I had just been released from the jaws of hell. The atmosphere in the hotel was something I can't describe other than that; it was as though I had gone in and out of a Dürer inferno.

We finally got the wall cleaned to the SS man's satisfaction, and to the wry amusement of I don't know how many passersby. Then he took our names and let us go, with the admonition that one more offense would result in arrest and imprisonment. We thanked him, and hurried off. The band was still playing.

We were silent for a long while, as we made our way toward Ole's uncle's house. Each one was reviewing in his mind what had just happened, and wondering if we hadn't misjudged the ease with which we could harass the Germans.

"It was an unlucky break," Ole said, at last. "If he hadn't been looking at us at just that instant, he'd never have caught us."

"Did you see him?" I asked.

"Of course not. I wouldn't have done it if I had."

It was a mildly unsatisfactory conclusion, and the only thing it taught us was that we'd have to be a great deal more careful in the future. Of course, if you're *too* careful you give yourself away by that very fact, so we had to strike a neat balance between being watchful and at the same time appearing not to be. It was a knack that took some little while to develop, and those who didn't perfect it were usually caught. And later on, of course, you weren't let off with a warning; you were shot.

As we neared the Amalienborg palace, we saw a sight that gave our spirits a much-needed lift. It had been the King's habit to ride through the streets of Copenhagen every day, alone on his bay horse and without any escort other than the people. (When the incredulous Germans asked a Dane who guarded him, the reply was, "We all do.") On the day of the invasion and the next day he didn't ride, but two days later he was out again, riding as though nothing had happened. Now we saw him, and behind him was a group of men and boys on bicycles, having a glorious time. The King was in uniform, his lean, wiry figure topped off with a tasseled cap on his head, and when people came into the street to greet him he smiled and shook their hands. His close-cropped moustache seemed to spread into his face when he smiled. You could feel in an almost tactile way the upsurge of morale that followed him, and those who greeted him seemed to be thanking him for bringing some cheer and pride back into their lives. It was a great moment, made even greater by his total ignoring of two German soldiers, who froze to attention and cracked their best salutes for him as he passed. He looked straight ahead, expressionless, and didn't smile again until he was well past them and greeting more of his countrymen. It was all so perfectly done that we found ourselves laughing. Ten minutes earlier, I'd have sworn I'd never laugh again.

Ole's uncle's shop was in a small street off Store Kongensgade, one of the many little finger streets that run up toward the railroad tracks. It was lined with food stores, dusty antique shops, and stores that displayed assorted doorknobs, pipes, and ship models. There was a large key hanging over the door of Ole's uncle's. We went inside and a bell tinkled, and in a minute a small, owlish man appeared. "What can I do for you?" he asked.

"It's me, Uncle Mogens," Ole said. "Ole Suensen."

"Ole!" his uncle said, peering through his glasses. "I didn't recognize you, you've grown so tall. Who's your friend?"

Ole introduced me, then cleared his throat and said, "Uncle Mogens, I was wondering if I could borrow a master key for a little while. I'll bring it back tonight."

His uncle blinked. "A master key to what? For what?"

Ole cleared his throat again. "Well, Jens and I have something we have to do at school, only it's locked today, so we need a master key to get in."

"What's so important it can't wait until Monday?"

"Uh—well, it's just—it's hard to explain."

"Try."

"That's about all I can tell you."

His uncle shook his head. "No go," he said. "I'm not going to be a party to any crime."

"It's not a *crime*, Uncle Mogens, it's just—"

"Taking a peek at some exam papers?"

"Lord, no! That would be cheating. This is all aboveboard—well—it certainly is no crime."

"Then tell me."

Ole took a deep breath, glanced at me, and then explained our idea. When he was finished, his uncle began to rummage through a drawer.

"Why didn't you say so in the first place?" he asked.

"I didn't know if you'd approve," Ole replied.

"If you young people would have a little more faith in your elders, things would be a lot easier," his uncle said. "Here you waste the time of day blathering on about nothing, when you could be up there cutting those stencils." He produced a bunch of keys and began to flip through them. "How do you plan to distribute the papers?"

"We thought of throwing them from the rooftops," Ole said.

"That won't cover much area." His uncle took three keys from the bunch, and handed them to Ole. "Better leave them on trams and buses and things like that, where they'll get a wider distribution. One of those keys ought to take care of any lock you come across."

"Thank you, Uncle Mogens," Ole said, grinning. "Thank you very much."

His uncle waved a hand in dismissal. "It's the least I can do," he said. "If I were twenty years younger I'd be out with you, but now I can't run fast enough. I'd be caught in no time flat." He paused. "By the way, do you know about sugar in the gas?"

Ole stared at him. "What do you mean?"

"Dump a little sugar in the gas tanks of their cars. It dissolves, and mucks up the engine to a fare-thee-well. The engines have to be all taken down and scoured."

Ole laughed. "Thank you. I'll remember that."

"If you pee in the gas tank it does the same thing," his uncle went on. "But of course that takes a little longer, and you're not in as good position to run if someone comes. Sugar is the quickest and best."

"Uncle Mogens, may I ask you a question?" Ole said.

"Of course."

"How is it you settled on being a locksmith? It seems to me there's a great future for you in other fields."

His uncle looked out the window. "Sometimes I ask myself the same thing," he said. "But there's more demand for locksmiths than there is for—ah—saboteurs, and this way I can sleep nights. If I were out raising hell around town, I'd always be wondering if someone was going to come to my house in the middle of the night and beat me up. Basically, I guess I'm a coward."

"Did you ever think of being an inventor?"

"My boy, I could take you to the basement and show you some of the things I've invented, and you wouldn't believe it. I have invented almost everything except the biplane, and a couple of Americans beat me to that. I invented a reversible can opener, which reseals the can after you've opened it. I invented a device for closing the window on cold mornings without getting out of bed. I invented a combination radio and toothbrush, so you can hear the news while the water's running. My greatest triumph was the silent alarm clock, but I was never able to market it."

"What do you mean, silent alarm clock?"

"It was a device to wake you only, without waking whoever was sleeping nearby."

"How did it work?"

Uncle Mogens coughed. "It was in suppository form. At the appointed hour, it fluttered."

Ole was stunned with admiration. "If we need any ideas, may we come to you?" he asked.

"By all means. Any time. I'd consider it an honor."

We turned to go, and Ole said, "Thank you again, Uncle Mogens."

"My pleasure," Uncle Mogens replied. "Have faith."

The school building was dim and quiet, and it smelled of furniture polish and chalk dust. Yellow window shades had been pulled halfway down, casting an amber light on everything, and our footsteps rang in the bare corridors. When we reached the office the first two keys we tried didn't fit, and for a moment I thought the whole thing was going to be for nothing. But the third key opened the door, and we were in. I found the drawer where the mimeograph stencils were kept, and while I began laboriously to peck out the message on a typewriter, Ole scoured around for paper. He could find only one package of blank sheets, so he made up the rest by using the backs of bulletins, schedules, and whatever else was lying around. By the time we were ready to start mimeographing, he had a respectable pile.

I was inking the roller, prior to cranking the first sheet

through, when we heard shuffling footsteps in the corridor, and then a key turned in the lock and the door opened, and there stood old Emil Lund, the janitor. His eyes were milky, and his hands looked like claws.

"What are you doing here?" he demanded. "Who are you?"

"Take it easy, Emil," Ole replied. "We're not hurting anything."

"What are you doing?" Emil moved closer, peering at the sheets.

"We're just knocking out a few copies of a schedule," Ole told him. "It's the soccer games for this spring."

"Those were posted last week," Emil said. "What are you doing?"

"Do you really want to know?" Ole asked. "Do you feel you won't sleep a wink tonight unless we enlighten you?"

"Crank a sheet through," Emil told me, and I looked at Ole, shrugged, and turned the crank. Emil picked up the sheet and read it, moving his lips as he did.

"Now are you satisfied?" Ole said.

"Where'd this come from?" Emil asked.

"It came through the mail," I replied. "We're just helping get the word around."

Emil put down the sheet. "A pack of lies," he said.

"I tell you, Emil," said Ole, "these days it's hard to know what are lies and what aren't, so we figure it's best the people have a lot of versions to choose from. Does that make sense to you?"

"Nothing makes sense," said Emil, and he shuffled out the door. Ole looked after him as he went.

"Do you think he recognized us?" I asked.

"No," said Ole. "He's been here so long all students look alike to him. He wouldn't be able to pick us out of a lineup of nuns."

"Well, anyway, he's harmless," I said. "He probably doesn't even know about the invasion."

Ole laughed. "There's always someone who doesn't get the word. On Tuesday afternoon, when the city was crawling with Germans, a guy showed up at my father's office and said, 'What's new?' Nobody can figure out how he'd got there without seeing a German, but he had."

"I hope your father told him, 'Nothing much,'" I said.

"My father was so stunned he didn't know how to begin. And speaking of beginning, let's get with these sheets. We haven't got all day."

In all, we made about two hundred and fifty copies, using every piece of paper we could lay our hands on. Then came the problem of how to transport them. We'd be fairly conspicuous lugging them in our arms, and we looked around and finally found a carton in which textbooks had been delivered. We filled the bottom of the carton with our sheets, then we put a layer of books on top of them and were ready to go. One person could carry the whole load, although before long it seemed much heavier.

We closed the office door behind us, and as the lock clicked I remembered I'd left the stencil on the roller. I was carrying the carton, and I held it out to Ole and said, "Take this and give me the key. I forgot the stencil."

"What difference?" he replied. "Who cares who sees it now?"

"Mightn't they trace it?"

"How? You didn't put your name on it."

"Still . . ." I didn't know why, but I hated to leave it behind.

"Come on, let's get out of here," Ole said. "I've got a creepy feeling in my spine."

I followed him as he let us out the side door, and we had started around toward the street when Ole suddenly whirled, flung himself at me, and pushed me back. "Gestapo!" he said in a whisper. We turned and raced across the yard, and flung ourselves down in some bushes at the edge of the soccer field. I was gasping for breath, and my arms ached from the weight of the carton.

"Where were they?" I asked, when I could talk.

"Just coming up. A big, black Mercedes, and three goons in trench coats. That son of a bitch Emil must have called them."

We waited for what seemed like hours but was probably only a half hour, and then we saw the black Mercedes pull away from the school and disappear. Carefully, looking in all directions, we crept off, and didn't stand upright until we were out of sight of the school. Then we walked to a corner and boarded the next tram that came along. I was still weak with fright, and would have given up the whole idea if Ole hadn't carried on as though nothing had happened. His sole concern was what to do about Emil.

"He's going to be a problem," he said, gazing out the window of the tram. "We're going to have to do something about him."

"Like what?" I asked.

"I don't know. We'll just have to see."

We rode to the next stop, left a few sheets behind us as we got off, and boarded the next car coming in the opposite direction. This way we crisscrossed the city, until our money was almost gone and only about a dozen sheets were left. We took a car to Town Hall Square and got off there, leaving the carton, the books, and the sheets on board. Then we split and went to our respective homes.

When I got home the blackout curtains were up, and my mother had lighted the candles. My father was sitting in his chair, reading the paper, and in the kitchen the radio was playing. He looked at me as I came in, and said, "Well?"

"Well what?" I asked, hanging up my coat.

"Did you manage to stay out of trouble?"

I gave him my injured innocence look. "What kind of trouble could *I* get into?" I said.

"I don't know. But it never hurts to ask."

"Yes, I stayed out of trouble," I replied, surreptitiously knocking wood.

And we left it at that.

Chapter Three

The chain letters continued, always in the same pale blue envelopes, and they gave a nice balance to the news. Our newspapers and radio, as I said, were censored, and you can be sure we got no news from the one daily and two weekly Nazi papers that were published in Copenhagen, so in the beginning we had to rely on the chain letters and the British Broadcasting Corporation for our news. The BBC was of immense help throughout the war, but more about that later.

About the Nazis: The Nazi Party in Denmark was small, numbering only a few thousand people, but they were noisy, and their leader, Frits Clausen, tried to think of himself as a budding Hitler. He had a large, bulbous jaw, a small mouth, and a low forehead above small, dark-ringed eyes, and he liked to be photographed in uniform, riding a horse. Most of the time, however, he wore civilian clothes. One of his main problems, aside from the fact that the great majority of Danes didn't take him seriously, was that Gen. von Kaupisch, the first German commander in Denmark, despised the Danish Nazis, and Gen. Lüdke, his successor, didn't think much more of them. This left Clausen with a lot of strutting and very little muscle.

And of course the Germans had their own problems. In spite of their earnest desire to be loved, they were bucking the fact that most Danes feared "the German inside the German," so no amount of sweet talk was wholeheartedly believed. And the Danish Cold Shoulder worked better than expected; Germans started complaining that the Danes didn't see them, and this kind of complaint, coming from members of the master race, had a strangely petulant sound. The majority Danish feeling was expressed by a fishwife, who said, "I would sooner have British bombs dropping around me than German. I think there's more good purpose in them, and that would make me feel safer." There were many exceptions, especially when the Germans were winning, but taken as a whole that summed up the Danish approach as well as anything. The Danish Government, however, was committed to a policy of collaboration, so in the beginning any anti-German acts were punished by our own police.

In short, everybody had a hard time.

Ole and I were frustrated by no longer being able to use the school's mimeograph machine, and hard as we tried we couldn't find another. Then, to make matters worse, printed handbills began to appear—posted on the sides of buildings, left on park benches and in trams and buses—and it was just the kind of thing we would have liked to be doing. These handbills went beyond just giving the news; they incited to sabotage, and Ole and I ground our teeth in envy every time we saw one. For obvious reasons the authors kept their identities secret, and Ole and I had no way to volunteer to help.

"I'm going to find out," he said one day, as we were reading a handbill we'd found stuck to my bicycle. "If it takes me all year, I'm going to find out. These guys have a real print-ing press, so that ought to give us a clue."

"I guess the Germans would like to know, too," I said. "They're probably just as eager as you are."

He thought for a few moments, then said, "I wonder."

"What?" It always made me cautious when Ole got that tone in his voice.

"I wonder if we were to volunteer to work for the Ger-mans—pretend we were Nazis—then they might send us to look for this press. . . ."

"Ole, you're out of your mind!" I said. "What makes you think they'd fall for a thing like that?"

"I didn't say they'd fall for it," he replied. "I was just exploring the possibilities."

"Let's just do a little sabotage, and let it go at that." As usual, his one wild idea had led me to settle for a lesser one, but wilder than I'd originally intended.

"All right," he said. "Like what?"

"I don't care. Whatever seems convenient."

We drifted toward the d'Angleterre, looking for unat-tended German automobiles, and Ole said, "Have you tried any sugar in the gas?"

"No," I replied. "With the rationing on, my mother keeps a strict eye on the sugar." (Rationing of certain foods, tobacco, and gasoline had been introduced, and while the food situation wasn't critical it was irritating. The smokers began to go crazy on imitation tobacco, and the automobilists were finally forced to use either horse-drawn or woodburning cars.)

"I filched some from a restaurant," said Ole. "It's in those little bags, so I can keep it in my pocket. As a matter of fact—" He looked up the block, withdrew an envelope from his pocket, and tore off a corner "—there's a nice big Mer-cedes there, that's just aching for some sugar."

I looked where he'd indicated, and there was indeed a Mer-cedes, but from my angle I could see there was a driver sitting behind the wheel. "Forget it," I said. "There's someone in it."

"I've already opened the package," said Ole. "We can't waste a whole thing of sugar."

I stared at him. "So?"

"So you engage him in conversation, while I drop the sugar in."

"*Me?* What do I say to him?"

"Anything that comes into your head."

We were now getting close to the car, and my heart began its familiar pounding. "Ole, remember what the SS man said—" I began, trying not to sound like a totally craven coward.

"Oh, very well, I'll talk to him," Ole said disgustedly, as he handed me the sugar. "You throw it in."

I took the packet as though it were an asp, and I watched Ole move up toward the driver's window. Hurriedly, trying to keep out of range of the rearview mirror, I unscrewed the gas cap, dropped the sugar in, bag and all, and closed the cap again. Then, breathing deeply to calm my trembling, I went to where Ole was talking with the driver.

"Well, what do you know about that?" I heard Ole saying. "I thought all Germans had to know how to yodel."

"Only in the Alps," the driver told him. "The Bavarians. And of course the Austrians can do it, too, but—" He shrugged, thereby dismissing the Austrians. "And the Swiss," he added. "But they don't count. The Bavarians are the only ones who really know how." His eyes flicked to me, and I had the terrible feeling he was reading my mind.

"This is my friend, Manfred," Ole said. "He tried to yodel once, but it made his nose bleed."

The driver looked at me as though I were a bug on a pin. Then he shook his head. "Not strong enough," he said. "He needs more chest."

"That's what I keep telling him," Ole replied. "But he won't do his exercises."

I nudged Ole hard, and said, "Come on. We're going to be late."

"Oh, all right," he replied, and then, to the driver, "It's been nice talking with you." The driver nodded, and we moved off.

"Damn it, Ole," I said, when we were out of hearing, "you're going to get in trouble some day."

"Like what?" He seemed genuinely surprised.

"You can't clown around with these people like that. You may think they're stupid, but they're not all *that* stupid."

"Why not?" said Ole. "We got away with it, didn't we? Besides, it was fun."

"For you, maybe. But you're not always going to get away with it."

"You sound like an old lady," said Ole, and that ended the conversation. Of course I was right; the time came when he didn't get away with it, but being right didn't make me feel any better when it happened.

We reached Strøget and turned left, and when we came to Kongens Nytorv we saw a strange thing. The band was playing as before, but now, instead of walking through the square, the Danes were avoiding it completely. There wasn't a single civilian in sight, and there was a slightly frantic note in the noise the musicians were making. I say "musicians" because in a technical sense that's what they were, but their output was about as musical as a train wreck. It might have sounded good to German ears, but to ours it was poison. (And if you ask how one can be poisoned through the ears, I refer you to King Hamlet of Denmark, whose brother dispatched him in just that manner.) Ole and I smiled at each other, then turned and walked away from the square.

We were retracing our steps down Strøget when we saw

three German soldiers coming out of a store. They wore fatigue caps and they were laughing, and one of them had the butt of a cigar clamped between his grinning teeth. It looked as though they had cleaned out the store; they were carrying so much that their various bundles had to be tied together with string, and one of them, a tall, thin youth with glasses, was festooned fore and aft with garlands of packages. There may have been rationing for us, but there was certainly none for them. They were making up for the last few years they'd spent in a country preparing for war, and were literally gorging themselves. In any other circumstances it would have been a pleasant sight—three jolly soldiers on a buying spree —but as matters stood it was simply one more insult. And to make matters worse they were doing it on credit; by the end of the Occupation, the German debt to Denmark was twelve billion kroner.

Ole and I watched them, and I could see his jaws tighten. I was afraid he was going to try to trip them up, or make some equally stupid move, but instead he waited until they'd passed, and then spat on the sidewalk. "And that's about the way I feel," he said, as we moved off. "As futile as a blob of spit."

"What do you mean?" I asked.

"These things we're doing—these pointless little jokes— they're not getting anywhere. They're not even pinpricks."

"Well, be realistic," I said. "The two of us can't take the place of an armored division."

"No, but we can do a lot better than pulling distributor wires and putting sugar in the gas."

"Like what?"

"Well, like—like if we could get hold of some explosives. *Then* we might be able to do something."

"And where do we get the explosives?"

He shrugged. "I don't know. Steal them, I guess."

"Where?"

"I said I don't know. I just know we have to do more than we're doing."

I thought for a while, and wondered what I'd do with a package of explosives if I had it. The thought was unsettling, but at the same time there was some excitement to it, because there was no denying what we were doing now was little better than common mischief-making. And to be arrested for a thing like that would be mortifying beyond belief. If we were going to be arrested—God forbid—it should be for something worthy of the punishment. The only problem was to find the material.

"Paraffin is a good igniter," Ole said, as though reading my thoughts. "You pour a lot of paraffin around and then touch it off, and you've got quite a brisk blaze going."

"As in for instance where?" I said.

"That's the problem. We've got to damage the Germans without damaging Danish property, and at the moment they're hard to separate."

"I have no doubt an idea will come," I said.

Just as we were entering Town Hall Square I saw Ingrid Nielsen, the girl I'd wanted to ask to the opening of Tivoli. Ingrid was not a blonde, like so many Danish girls; her hair was a sort of chestnut color with a slight tinge of red, and although not too tall she had the longest legs of any girl I'd ever seen. She seemed to flow rather than walk, and more than once she reminded me of Hans Andersen's Little Mermaid. Conversely, whenever I saw the Little Mermaid, on her rock at the harbor entrance, I thought of Ingrid. I'd spoken to her only in passing; whenever I'd been close enough there was always another boy around, and he was never welcoming. Now, however, she was alone, and for the first time since the invasion I thought about my birthday. It seemed a lot less important than it had, but the sight of Ingrid made the whole thing suddenly more appealing.

"Hey, Ingrid!" I called, and waved.

She looked at me, and I saw her look at Ole, and then she stopped and smiled as we approached. "Hello," she said, in a soft voice.

"Hi," said Ole, and for a second I hated him. The way he said it indicated he knew her a great deal better than I did.

"I haven't seen you in quite a while," I told her. "Where've you been keeping yourself?"

"Here and there," she replied. "Why?" I got the feeling she was talking to Ole while looking at me.

"I was wondering if you were busy on the first," I said, speaking so fast I was barely intelligible.

"The first of May?" Her eyes, which were light blue-green, looked at something over my shoulder, then back at me.

"Yes. It's the opening of Tivoli."

"So it is." A pause of perhaps two seconds. "No, I'm not doing anything."

"Would you come with me?"

"I'd love to."

It seemed unbelievable. "That's great!" I said. "I'll pick you up—uh—when would you like?"

"Whenever you say." She appeared to be smiling, although her mouth didn't change.

"How about—ah—seven?"

"Seven it is." She started off.

"Wait a minute," I said, putting out a hand. "Where do you live?"

"Smedegade 37," she replied. "I'm sorry to rush, but I'm late."

"How do I get there?"

"Ole can tell you." And she was gone.

"It's not hard," Ole said. "You go across Gyldenløvesgade Bridge to Blaagaardsgade, take a right, and it's your first right after that."

"Thanks a lot," I said sourly.

He looked at me. "What's the matter with you?"

"Nothing. Why?"

"You sound sore."

"What would I be sore at?"

"Don't ask *me*."

"Then don't say I'm sore."

"I didn't; I said you *sounded* sore."

"The same thing."

This idiotic exchange went on until neither of us could think of anything more to say, and by that time my pique had worn off. But, since I didn't want to admit I'd been in a pique in the first place, I took a little longer than necessary denying it. Finally we subsided, and ambled along in silence for a while. Then I said, "How well do you know her?"

"Who?" said Ole.

"Ingrid! Who do you think we've been talking about?"

"We were last talking about you."

"Well, now we're talking about Ingrid! How long have you known her?"

"How long? Oh, maybe two–three years, on and off."

"What do you mean, on and off?"

"Just that. Here and there."

"How well do you know her?"

"Why? What do you want to know?"

"I want to know how *well* you know her! I want to know what to expect!"

Ole looked into the distance for what seemed to me a long time. "I hardly know what to tell you," he said, at last. "Sometimes she's one thing, sometimes she's another."

"Great," I said. "That's a big help."

"It's all I can tell you. If I try to be specific, she's apt to make a liar out of me."

It began to sound as though I'd contracted to take a chameleon to the opening of Tivoli. "I guess I'll have to find out for myself," I said, as though it were some great imposition.

"I guess you will," said Ole. "If what you've been trying to say is can you hold hands or something with her, all I can tell you is I wouldn't be surprised. Beyond that, you're on your own."

"Ah, well," I said, wishing I'd never brought the subject up, "I suppose there's such a thing as knowing too much in advance, anyway."

"That's right," said Ole. "Keep a little suspense in your life, and you'll have more fun."

I hadn't had enough experience with girls to be sure of myself in any conditions, much less the uncertain ones forecast by Ole. I began almost to regret I'd asked her for the date. And the fear of failure had removed from me any desire other than that of having as relaxed and cheerful an evening as possible. All in all, my seventeenth birthday shaped up as a potential disaster of major proportions.

She lived on the other side of Peblinge Sø, an extension of the Sortedams Sø near which we lived, and using Ole's directions I found her house with no trouble. I was, in fact, ten minutes early, so I walked back to the water and looked at the blacked-out city, with its spires and towers and turrets silhouetted against the evening sky. For the first time, I became fully aware of what was happening to us: The whole country, which just over three weeks ago had been at peace with the world, was now a passive if unwilling part of a monstrous war machine, and the tiny protests that people like Ole and me were making were less than ineffectual; all they could ever accomplish would be to make the authorities irritated, and therefore meaner. Any effective resistance would have to be widespread and coordinated, and at the time that was simply out of the question. What we'd have to do, little by little, was build up an organization, and how we would go about that was beyond my comprehension. It was one thing to say it, and quite another thing to do it. It made me feel small, and alone, and frustrated, but the frustration brought on an anger that kept the resolve alive. If I hadn't felt the frustration I'd probably have been resigned, but the two feelings simply do not go together.

It was in this somewhat prickly mood that I returned to Ingrid's house to pick her up. I knocked, and after a few moments she opened the door. I couldn't see her face because the light was behind her, but I could detect a cleanly-washed, cosmetic smell about her, mixed with a musky perfume. (At that point soap rationing had not yet had its effect, and people were able to stay clean.)

"My, but you're prompt," she said, holding the door open.

"Never keep a lady waiting," I replied, in what I hoped was a gallant tone.

"Shut the door, you're showing a light!" came a loud voice from inside.

"Yes, Dada," she replied, and then, to me, "Come in, and meet my father."

I stepped inside, blushing slightly. I don't know why, but hearing other people's family nicknames is always embarrassing to me, as though I'm listening to something I shouldn't be in on. Someone the size of Ingrid calling someone else "Dada" threw everything out of kilter for me. She took me into the living room, where her father was sitting surrounded by as many candles as if he'd been in a coffin. A newspaper lay in his lap, and he looked at me over the tops of his glasses.

"Dada, this is Jens Hansen," she said, and again I squirmed.

"Good evening, sir," I said.

Mr. Nielsen examined me for a few moments more, then grunted. "Where are you going?" he asked.

"Tivoli, sir," I replied. "It's opening night."

"See you're back early."

"Yes, sir." I didn't know what he meant by early, but I wasn't going to argue.

"And see you don't do anything funny."

"Sir?" I didn't know if he was referring to my conduct with Ingrid, or what.

"I don't want my daughter mixed up in anything."

"No, *sir*." Again, his meaning was vague, but I was willing to agree.

" Do you know what I mean?"

"Ah—yes, sir."

"What?"

"Well—you don't want her—uh—mixed up."

"I don't want her involved in anything shady."

"With *me*? Mr. Nielsen, I'm a—"

"I hear a lot of you young people are sneaking around trying to do things that upset the Germans. I want my daughter to have no part in that."

I glanced at the paper in his lap to see if by any chance it was one of the Nazi publications, and was relieved to see it wasn't. "I don't go in for that kind of thing, sir," I said. "I believe in live and let live."

"We're going to coexist with the Germans until they've won this war, and the less we irritate them the happier we'll all be." He shook the kinks out of his paper, and went back to reading it as though I weren't there. But he'd said the one thing that triggered a reaction in me, and in spite of myself I heard myself replying.

"Are you sure they're going to win it, sir?" I said, and behind me I could hear Ingrid stop breathing. Her father looked up at me coldly.

"Aren't you?" he asked.

"No, sir."

"Why not?"

"Well—just because we gave in, it doesn't mean everybody else will."

"The Poles and the Norwegians tried to fight, and look what it got them." (By now, all organized resistance in Norway had come to an end.)

"Yes, sir, I know. But—"

"The German Army is the greatest military machine ever developed. The Luftwaffe alone can conquer any country in Europe. If the British and French are stupid enough to fight, they'll be destroyed." He returned to his paper, but I was trembling with rage and beyond control.

"If you'd care to make a bet, sir—" I began, and then Ingrid grabbed me by the arm and hustled me out of the room.

"You shouldn't have done that," she told me, when we got outside. "You should always agree with him."

I took several deep breaths. "I'm sorry," I said. "I didn't mean to. It just happened."

"Mama and I stay out of the room while he's reading the paper. That's when he gets his most positive."

"Where was your mother tonight?"

"In the kitchen, listening to the radio. She always listens to the BBC, but she keeps it very soft."

Putting it as delicately as I could, I said, "Is your father in *favor* of the Germans, or does he just think they're going to win?"

It was a few moments before she answered. "He doesn't really like them," she said, at last. "But he considers himself a realist. He's decided they've already won, and that's all there is to it." She thought for another moment, and added, "And if there's anything he hates to be, it's wrong."

"I could see that," I said.

"You don't know the half of it." She laughed and slipped her arm through mine, and I felt hot flashes go all up and down my spine.

In peacetime, Tivoli is a riot of lights, music, fireworks, and flowers. Lights sparkle like stars in the trees, white lilacs appear to grow in and on everything, and the night air shudders and flashes with the bursting of huge chrysanthemums of colored fire. Needless to say there was none of this in 1940; all the lights had to be hooded so as not to show from above, and they made glowing pools in the darkness that, while not exactly festive, at least created a mysterious and slightly romantic atmosphere. It wasn't the Tivoli we knew, but it was better than nothing.

When we got on the dance floor, I noticed for the first time that she was wearing a knitted beret, or skull cap, on the back of her head. Her hair curled out and around it, so from the front you couldn't see it, but from any other angle you could see it was two concentric circles of blue and white, with a large red dot in the middle.

"That's a cute cap," I said, executing one of my better dips. "Did you make it?"

"No, I got it in school. You know what it is?"

I looked at it, so close to my eyes as almost to make me cross-eyed. Removing a little of her hair from my mouth, I said, "No. What?"

"The RAF."

I pulled away, and saw she was smiling at me. "Are you serious?" I asked.

"Of course. Lots of the girls have them."

"What does your father say?"

"You think I'm crazy? He's never seen it. I only wear it when I'm out of the house."

I laughed, and brought her head close to mine again. "That's the best I've ever heard. I'll have to think of something like that for myself."

"Some boys put them on their bikes," she said. "Either the RAF cockades, or little British flags. It's getting to be quite the thing. They also show Danish flags, but that's not quite so risky."

I thought of Ole's and my carryings-on, and how stupid it would be to call attention to ourselves with little flags, but I decided not to mention any of that. I was instinctively learning the first rule of underground activity, which is that the fewer people who know what you're doing, the better it is for all concerned. So I simply said, "I don't see that any of it's too risky, do you?"

"I guess we'll find out," she replied.

"I guess we will," I said, and concentrated on my dancing.

I honestly don't know where the rest of the evening went. All I know is that in what seemed like fifteen minutes she looked at her watch and said, "Uh-oh. It's almost midnight," and we got her coat and started home. The night air was soft, and the stars seemed unnaturally bright, and as we walked arm in arm through the darkened streets we chatted and joked and sang as though we'd known each other for years. When we neared her house she removed her beret, stuffed it in her coat pocket, and said, "This has been a lovely evening."

"I enjoyed it," I replied.

We were in front of her door, and she turned and faced me. "You know something?" she said.

"What?" I couldn't think what might be coming.

"You're different."

"Oh?" The way she said it, I couldn't tell if it was a compliment or not.

"Yes."

"In what way?"

"I'd spoil it if I told you."

"Is it good or bad?"

"Good."

"All right, then." I hesitated, then said, "May I say something?"

"Please do."

"This is the best birthday I've ever had."

She put her hands to her face. "This is your *birth*day?"

I nodded. "One seven."

"You should have *told* me!"

"What would you have done that you didn't?"

"Nothing, but—well, happy birthday!" She took my face in her hands and kissed me, and before I could get my arms around her she was in her door and gone. I stood there for several minutes, looking at the closed door, and then I turned and walked slowly toward my home, grinning like a clown.

Chapter Four

I met Ole after school the next day, and as we bicycled home he said, "How did it go?"

"How did what go?" I replied, knowing perfectly well what he meant.

"Your date."

"Oh—" I shrugged "—all right, I guess."

There was a silence, during which I had trouble keeping my face straight, and finally he said, "Get anywhere?"

"Depends on what you mean by anywhere."

Another silence. "In other words, you did all right."

"I guess you'd call it that."

We pedaled along for two blocks without talking, and then Ole said, "What kind of approach did you use?"

"I didn't use any." It was a long time since I'd enjoyed myself so much, and I wanted to keep the game going. "Everything sort of fell into place," I said.

"Lucky you," said Ole.

"You know how it is," I went on. "Sometimes things just drop in your lap."

"Not in mine, they don't," said Ole. "I have to work for every one of them."

"I know what you mean," I said, with what I hoped sounded like sympathy.

"It doesn't appear that way."

"I've had my troubles. Remember Herta Toksvig?" Herta was a blonde I'd taken on a double date with Ole and his then-girl, and somehow in all the scuffling I managed to step on her foot and crack one of the small bones. She never spoke to me again.

Ole laughed. "I remember," he said. "That was a bad night."

"I've had my share of them," I said.

"But not last night."

"That's right."

Ole sighed. "Son of a gun," he said.

I felt we'd milked the subject for all it was worth, and I was now even with him for his evasiveness, so I said, "You mentioned earlier you had an important bit of news. What is it?"

"Oh. That." Ole looked around to see if there was anyone in hearing distance, then said, "I know where we can get some explosives."

My stomach jumped. "Where?"

"There's a construction company working on the road down by Dragør. They keep their dynamite locked in a shed, but I've got the key."

"Where'd you get it?"

"Uncle Mogens—where else?"

"What do you plan to do with it?"

"Open the shed, of course."

"I mean the dynamite."

"Oh. Well, I thought we should think about that. The best thing, of course, would be German headquarters, but I'm afraid that's a little risky."

"Glad to hear you say it," I replied. "I agree completely."

"So that leaves us with factories, or—I don't know."

"What factories?"

"Those producing goods for the Germans."

"How many are there?"

"I don't know. Only a few now, but there'll be more."

"I don't like the idea of bombing Danish property."

"Neither do I. But what else?"

"Do they have a motor pool? We could blow up a few of their trucks."

Ole thought about this. "Wire the dynamite to the starter, so it'd go off when the key turned. That way, you'd get the driver, too."

A bad taste began to develop in my mouth. "Let's think of something else," I said.

"Anyway," said Ole, "the first thing is to get the dynamite. After that, we can decide what to do with it."

"I guess so."

"How about tonight?"

I swallowed. "What'll I tell my parents?"

"Tell 'em you're coming over to my house, to play cards."

I'd never lied to them, and I didn't like to start now. "I'll just say I'm going out with you," I said.

"Say what you like. I'll meet you in Town Hall Square at—when? Eight?"

"OK."

"Eight it is." He veered off and pedaled down a side street, leaving me to ride home with my thoughts.

After supper, when my father had settled down with his paper, I looked at my watch and pretended surprise. "I didn't realize it was so late," I said, going to the coat rack.

"So late for what?" he asked, looking up.

"I've got to meet Ole at eight." I put on my coat, and knotted my scarf around my neck.

"To do what?"

"He has some project he wants me to help him with." I reached for my cap.

"A project such as what?"

"I don't know, exactly."

My mother came in from the kitchen. "Where are you going?" she asked.

"Nobody seems to know," my father told her. "He's meeting Ole Suensen on some clandestine mission."

"It is not clandestine!" I said, telling the first outright lie of the evening. "I simply don't know the details." This was, stretching the truth only slightly, correct, since we didn't yet know what to do with the dynamite. Also, I didn't know exactly where it was.

"It seems funny he wouldn't tell you," my mother said. "You and he seem to share in everything you do."

"He *will* tell me!" I protested. "It's just that I don't know all the details this very moment! Now, please—you sound as though I were going off on some sabotaging mission!"

"God forbid," said my father. "We've never had violence in this house."

"Well, you can tell us all about it when you get back," my mother said. "By then, you'll know what you were doing."

"That's right," I said, going to the door. "And now, if you'll excuse me, I don't want to be late."

"All I can say is it must be important," my father remarked.

As I closed the door behind me I heard my mother saying, "If you ask me, it'll turn out to have something to do with girls. It's hard to realize he's reached that age, but when I make his bed—" I closed the door and heard no more. It would have been easier, I reflected, to take Ole's suggestion and say we were going to play cards; by trying to stay close to the truth I'd let myself in for some really whopping lies later on.

Ole was waiting at the corner where the Vestre boulevard leaves the southern corner of Town Hall Square, and when he saw me coming he started on ahead, so that I caught up with him only gradually. We rode in silence across Langebro Bridge and headed down the island of Amager toward Kastrup Airport. I noticed he'd strapped a basket to the handlebars of his bicycle, and in it was a bundle I couldn't identify. Our ears were searching for any sound, either of boots or of an automobile, that would indicate a German patrol or prowl car, but all we heard was the hissing of our own tires and the distant barking of a dog. It's too early to be nervous now, I told myself; if anyone stopped us, they'd have no proof of anything. The really hairy ride is going to be the one back into town. I ran my tongue over my teeth, and felt a molar twinge with a sort of acidlike pain. Oh, fine, I thought. That's all I need now, is to have a tooth go bad.

Dragør lies beyond the airport, on the island that hangs like a punching bag into the Sound separating Denmark from Sweden. It is about eight and three-quarter miles from Copenhagen, but in all other respects it is light years away. It was originally settled in the Stone Age; during the Middle Ages it was very big in trade fairs, and in the sixteenth century a group of Dutch farmers and sea captains made it into a going concern as a seafaring town. Its atmosphere is mostly eighteenth-century Dutch: steep-gabled, red tile roofs; narrow, winding, cobblestone streets; a pair of operating town pumps; and a busy harbor, all so clean you could eat right off the ground. When we rode through, the only sound was the rattling of our bikes over the cobblestones, although somewhere I heard the hollow, wooden clump of a person walking in clogs. It didn't have the crack that boot heels make; it was an unmistakably civilian sound. And a comforting one.

We went through the town, and onto the road that skirts the shore. After over half a mile the ground got bumpy, and then we came on the construction area. Piles of rock and gravel loomed to one side, and a silent, tarpaulin-covered steamroller towered in the darkness like an elephant in a very small tent. We dismounted, and wheeled our bikes to where I could just make out a wooden shed, looking as innocent as a farmer's outhouse. Ole leaned his bike against it, took a flashlight from the basket, and, cupping his hand around the lens to make an absolute minimum of light, he produced a key and slipped it in the padlock, and in less than five seconds the hasp swung free. The door squeaked as we opened it, and to us it sounded as loud as the shriek of a banshee. We stopped, frozen, but there was no other sound, and after a moment we slipped inside.

The shed smelled of moist earth and the peculiar burnt-cork smell of dynamite. Ole flashed his light around, and we saw the workmen's shovels, pickaxes, and sledgehammers, and then, in one corner, a box half full of neatly piled dynamite sticks, each one about the size of a candle. Above it, on a nail, hung coils of fuse, and high on the opposite wall, in a small wooden box, were the fulminate-of-mercury detonators.

"We won't bother with them," Ole said, flicking his light on the detonators. "They're likely as not to go off in your pocket." He examined the dynamite, then picked up three sticks and handed them to me.

"You want me to put them in your basket?" I asked.

"Hell, no. We should both carry them, so if one of us gets caught the other will still have some. We don't want the trip to be a total loss." I coughed and put the sticks in my overcoat pocket, and he gave me three more. "Now take some fuse," he said, reaching for a coil, "and I'll do the same. A dozen sticks ought to keep us happy for a while."

"I guess that depends on what you mean by happy," I said.

Ole laughed. "There's nothing better than this," he replied, and at that moment I began to wonder if he wasn't perhaps the slightest bit crazy.

We left the shed and snapped the padlock shut, and Ole put his dynamite and other things in his basket, stuffing an old jacket on top of them to keep them from rattling. Then we wheeled our bikes to the road, mounted, and started off. We hadn't gone ten yards when from behind us someone shouted, "Hey! Who's there? Halt!" My skin froze, and I jumped so violently I almost fell off my bike, but I recovered my balance, leaned over the handlebars, and pedaled as I had never pedaled before. Ole and I raced, neck and neck, along the darkened road, and gradually the shouts faded away.

We rode as hard as we could for as long as we could, but inevitably we had to slow down. My legs were aching, and my chest felt bound by steel bands, and I was wet all over with the perspiration not only of exercise, but also of fear. I must have stunk like a goat.

"Where are we going to keep this stuff?" I asked Ole as we crossed Langebro.

"I've scooped out a place in a window box," he replied. "We'll bury it there, and take our time deciding what to do with it."

So we went to his house, unloaded our haul into the window box, and put the earth and red geraniums back over it. I rode slowly home, feeling weak and washed-out. It was slightly after ten, but the adrenalin was still pumping into my system, and tired as I was I didn't feel like sleeping. When I let myself in, my parents were waiting.

"Well!" my father exclaimed. "Now you can tell us all about it!"

I sank into a chair, trying to think of something to say, but my mind was bereft of ideas.

"Jens, you're as red as a beet!" my mother said. "What *have* you been doing?"

"Ole and I had a bicycle race," I replied, still instinctively clinging to the last shreds of the truth.

"At this hour of the night?" said my father. "Come on, boy, don't expect me to believe that."

"What difference does it make?" I asked.

"Mr. and Mrs. Bjøl came by," my mother put in. "They asked after you, and we didn't know what to tell them." Mr. and Mrs. Hans Bjøl lived down the street, and between them they gathered and disseminated more rumors and false stories than all the professional news services combined.

"Why couldn't you just tell them I was out?" I said.

"You know them," my mother replied. "They wanted to know all about you." She paused, and smiled. "I told them I thought you were out with a girl."

"You were right," I said, hating myself but at the same time seeing a way to bring the inquisition to a close.

"And I suppose she was in this bicycle race, too?" my father said.

I turned and looked at him, giving him what I hoped was a man-to-man look. "Yes," I said, slowly. "In a manner of speaking."

"And Ole?"

"Ole, I assume, is home in bed."

There was a silence, while my father and I looked into each other's eyes, and then my mother said, briskly, "Well, I'm sure it's none of our business, so we won't press the point. But I do wish next time you'd give us some hint of what you're doing. It's awfully hard for us to have to invent things."

"You do all right," I said, running my tongue over my

teeth and feeling the same twinge. I thought about the dentist, then decided the whole thing would be better tomorrow. Fright sometimes makes your teeth hurt, I told myself.

"My advice to you is to take a bath and go to bed," my mother said. "There's nothing so relaxing as a nice, hot bath."

"Thank you, Mother," I said, rising. "That's a good idea." And I went to the bathroom and drew a tub.

One week later, all hell broke loose. I should explain that the French, having been invaded by the Germans twice in less than forty-five years (and soundly trounced the first time), were understandably a little leery of their neighbors to the northeast. During the 1930's, one of their big thinkers named André Maginot decided that the best way to keep the Germans from spilling in again would be to build a line of forts along the Franco-German border, with concrete tank traps, long underground passages, and a system of interconnecting fire that would murder anyone who came near. So this line of forts was built and named after Maginot, and the French sat back and felt safe. What everyone knew, but didn't emphasize, was that the line stopped short of the Belgian border, because the French thought it would be insulting to their friends the Belgians to fortify the boundary between them. Now, pretend you're the Germans, and you want to get into France: Do you go and crack your heads against a line of supposedly impregnable forts, or do you execute a swift end run through the area where there are none? Exactly. And that's what they did, to the aggrieved astonishment of everyone, especially the French.

On May 10, 1940, the Germans bombed and blasted their way into the Netherlands, Belgium, and Luxembourg, and then came howling down into France, on almost exactly the route they'd taken in 1914. They got behind the Maginot Line (whose guns fired in only one direction) and wiped that out; they mangled the British and French armies and drove a third of a million of them into the sea at Dunkirk, where the survivors were rescued by a hastily gathered fleet of nine hundred boats and taken to England; and on June 22 they signed an armistice with the French Government, which had fled Paris and gone to Vichy. In not quite two months they had almost accomplished what they took four years trying, and failing, to do before.

You'll notice I said "almost." The British had been driven back across the Channel, but they hadn't given up, and on July 10 the Luftwaffe began a systematic bombing of England, to soften it up for invasion. Few people doubted the invasion would succeed; the only question seemed to be when it would come. In what became known as the Battle of Britain, the Germans mounted heavier and heavier raids, wiping out cities like Coventry and laying waste whole districts of London, Birmingham, and others. But the RAF made it so costly, in one case knocking down more than a hundred planes in one day, that the Germans finally gave up the effort, and by the end of the year they were turning their attention elsewhere. They had found out, as others were to find out later, that bombing civilians only stiffens their will to resist.

But during the period from May to July, and on into the autumn, they seemed invincible. There was no valid reason to hope the British would hold out, and in spite of all of Winston Churchill's brave words it seemed only a matter of time before they went under. The Nazis, both German and Danish, were naturally gleeful, and many Danes resigned themselves to living with the Germans as the new masters of Europe. Not many of them liked the idea, but there didn't seem to be much that could be done about it.

But not everyone was resigned. Among the Danish youth groups, plans were under way that fall for an organized resistance if the British should go down; the younger Danes felt we'd given in too quickly in the first place, and they were determined not to give in all the way. And of course the British never considered the idea of surrender. And here was where the BBC won its reputation for truth, because it never tried to gloss over the facts, or pretend that things were anything but terrible. They admitted their reverses and their defeats, but their attitude was simply that the more they lost now, the longer it would take them to win in the end. *They* had no doubt they'd win, and when you listen to people like that who are obviously telling the truth, it makes you wonder. The Nazis, on the other hand, kept blatting on about their glorious victories even when they'd started to lose, so nobody paid any attention to them. It was a remarkable thing: the engineers in the Copenhagen light and power company noticed a sharp upsurge at precisely six fifteen every evening; they were mystified until they realized that that was the hour when the BBC came on in Danish, and the 150,000 radio sets in the city were being turned on to listen.

During that long and depressing first summer of the war, the Danes had only two things to cheer them up: community singing, and the King. The King continued his daily rides, being warmly greeted wherever he went, and people seemed to cling to him as a symbol of national unity. And, in more or less the same way, community singing gave them something in common, and a way of expressing their patriotism without committing any overt acts of rebellion. Nobody paid any attention to the German band in Kongens Nytorv, but every so often people would gather in one of the parks, hundreds and thousands of people, and sing themselves hoarse with patriotic songs. It provided a great lift for the morale, and there was nothing the Germans could do about it. They even pretended to ignore the miniature British flags and RAF cockades, which appeared with increasing frequency and fairly burgeoned during the Battle of Britain. They were still clinging to their "systematisch beliebt" charade, and trying to be good eggs about it all. When, finally, they dropped the mask, they made up for lost time, but that wasn't for more than three years.

One of the greatest mass demonstrations I've ever seen occurred on Thursday, September 26, which was the King's seventieth birthday. Ole and I were now in our senior year in school, but there was no school that day, and we joined the crowds of people who, with no instructions and nobody to lead them, just naturally began to gravitate toward Amalienborg. They surrounded the palace, they clogged the streets leading toward it, and they had Danish flags and Allied flags and RAF colors (it was at the height of the Battle of Britain), and they sang so loudly I didn't think there'd be an unruptured larynx in the city of Copenhagen. Ole and I sang until our throats were sore, and just when I thought I couldn't make another peep the palace gates swung open, and out came the King. I'm not ashamed to say I wept, as did a lot of others, and I shrieked so loud I finally was smitten mute. My whole voice box just gave out. The king rode along, smiling and saluting, and people reached up to touch him and hold his stirrups, and just be near him, and then the crowd began to follow him as he rode through the streets. It was as though they'd all gone wild; you'd think the war had suddenly ended, the way they carried on. Ole and I followed along and then, croaking like frogs and feeling emotionally washed out, we drifted away and let others take our place.

We were silent for a few minutes and then, whispering because it was the only way he could talk, Ole said, "Seen much of Ingrid lately?"

I shook my head. I'd seen her once or twice since our date in May, but world events had taken precedence over everything else, and all other things seemed somehow unimportant. Even Ole's and my dynamite, which we'd gone through so much to acquire, still lay buried in his window box for the simple reason that, in the face of everything else that was happening, twelve sticks of dynamite seemed so piddling as to be pointless. We didn't doubt we'd use them, but nothing we thought of seemed quite right.

"I thought I might give it a try," Ole whispered. "If that's all right with you."

"Why ask me?" I rasped. "You knew her first." I felt a pang of jealousy, but in all honesty there was nothing I could object to. He *had* known her first, and as a suitor I'd been woefully remiss. That was the story of my life with girls: something always happened to keep me from following up whatever good impression I might have made in the beginning. Once it was mumps, another time it was Herta Toksvig's foot, and so on. There were times when I wondered if I'd ever get married. Now, suddenly, Ingrid seemed wildly desirable.

"Well, we'll see," said Ole. "I can't do anything about it until I can talk again."

I didn't want to wish him anything bad, but it would have been all right with me if he hadn't been able to speak for a month. As this churlish thought was running through my mind, I realized that my tooth was hurting again, and I wondered if emotion had anything to do with it. It had given me twinges at various times during the summer, but they were never bad enough to make me take the fatal step of telling my parents. That, I knew, would lead to the dentist, which was to be avoided at almost all costs. Now, however, the ache was more persistent, and I had the trapped feeling that comes with the knowledge that the time for stalling has passed. I touched my tongue to the tooth, and was rewarded with a jolt that made the whole jaw ache. Oh, Lord, I thought. I guess this time I'm in for it.

When I got home I told my mother about seeing the King, and all the attendant excitement, and then, taking a deep breath, I said in my croaking voice, "Is Dr. Hasselriis still in business?"

"I presume so," she replied. "Why?"

Even now I was reluctant to admit the trouble, so I said, "No reason. I just wondered."

"Is something wrong?"

I shrugged. "I can't be sure."

"You wouldn't have mentioned it otherwise."

"All right, then, yes. I have a toothache."

"Why didn't you say so?" She went to the telephone and made a call, waited a few moments, then hung up. "No answer," she said, picking up the telephone book. "How long has it been bothering you?"

"On and off."

She flicked through the phone book. "I said how long?"

"Well . . . since May."

She gave me a horrified look, made another call, and waited. Again, no answer. "I tell you what," she said. "There's a dental clinic on Kronprinsessegade. Go on over there, and they'll take care of it for you. If this has been going on since May . . ." She left the sentence unfinished.

At any other time I'd have stalled until our regular dentist was available, but by now my jaw was beginning to throb, and I wanted to get it over with. I put on my cap and went out.

It was one of those beautiful days in early autumn, when the trees are changing color and the sky is clean and crisp. Since Denmark is bounded on virtually every side by water, it inherits its weather from the sea, and to the north was a towering pile of cottony clouds that gave one the feeling of being far out on the ocean. I thought how wonderful it would be, first to have my tooth stop pounding, then to have the war ended, and finally to be on a ship at sea with Ingrid. Any one of the conditions would be nice, but all three together would be unutterable bliss. I wished I'd been a little more attentive to her in recent weeks, and vowed to look into the matter as soon as I could.

I climbed the stairs to the dental clinic, each step making my tooth pulse like a boil, and tried the door. It was locked, and I rang the bell, by now terrified that I'd never be able to find help. I heard the sounds of rapid movement inside, and several sets of footsteps, and then the door opened a crack, and a man in a white jacket looked out.

"Sorry, we're busy," he said, and started to close the door.

"Wait a minute," I pleaded. "This is an emergency. Please—I need help."

He stopped, and peered at me. "What's the matter?"

In contrast to the way I'd presented the case to my mother, I now went all out. "I've got a tooth that's been infected since last spring," I said. "It's killing me—I think my whole jaw is infected. It's probably got to my brain." This was quite a speech considering the condition of my voice, and the man hesitated a moment more, then opened the door.

"Come in," he said. "I have a patient in the chair, but I'll see you right after him."

I went into the waiting room, where two men were reading dog-eared magazines, and neither of them looked at me as I sat down. The dentist went into an adjoining room and closed the frosted glass door behind him, and after a few moments the door opened and another man came out, adjusting his necktie. The dentist appeared behind him, beckoned to me, and then said to the two waiting men, "I hope you gentlemen don't mind if I see this young man first. It seems to be something of an emergency."

"Not in the least," said one of them. "Go right ahead."

"I've got all day," said the other. "Don't hurry for me."

Now, I know that Danes are cheerful and polite, and I know that nobody is in a hurry to sit in a dentist's chair, but the behavior of these two men struck me as downright odd. I sat in the chair, and while the dentist was washing his hands I thought about this, but I came to no conclusion other than I'd been lucky getting in so quickly.

The dentist put a bib around my neck, and as he did he said, "In the future, it would be a help if you'd call before you come."

"I'm sorry," I said. "My mother tried, but got no answer."

He seemed to frown at this, then peered into my mouth. "Wow," was all he said.

What had happened, briefly, was that air had leaked under a filling; in time the air had caused decay to set in, and the decay finally turned to infection. The dentist gave me a shot of novocaine and set to work.

I've always been interested in the various tools people use in their professions, and at one point, when the dentist had turned for a new drill, I sat upright and scanned the tray in front of my face. There was the usual alcohol burner, and jar of cotton, and the forceps and probe and mirror, and then there was something halfway under the paper doily. I picked it up and examined it, and as I was turning it over in my hands the dentist saw me, and jumped and snatched it away.

"Don't touch anything!" he said, sharply. "Where'd you find that?"

"On the tray," I replied, flinching.

"Keep your hands off the tray," he said, and then, more gently, "Let me know if this hurts."

It did hurt, because with the infection the novocaine wasn't a hundred per cent effective, so he gave me another shot, and then everything was all right. Actually, my mind was so busy I was almost above pain, because what I'd picked from the tray was a small slug of type, the kind that's set by hand, and the only reason I recognized it was that my father had once taken me on a tour of his paper and a man in the composing room had given me a slug as a souvenir. Slowly it came to me, as I reviewed everything I'd seen and heard since entering the clinic, that something more than dentistry was going on here. I tried to catch the dentist's eye, to see if I could get some acknowledgment, but he studiously avoided looking at me, and I knew better than to ask any outright questions. Then, finally, he was finished.

"That ought to be all right in a few days," he said. "If it doesn't clear up you can call me, and I'll take a look at it."

"Yes, sir," I said. "Thank you." My lips and cheek were numb, and felt like cotton to the touch.

"What happened to your voice?" he asked.

"It's the King's birthday," I replied. "I got carried away, and cheered too loud."

He smiled, and this time our eyes met. "Remember to call before you come," he said.

"Yes, sir," I replied. "I will."

I put on my cap and left the clinic, and went as fast as I could to find Ole.

Chapter Five

I didn't find him until the next day, when we were on our way to school. "Where were you yesterday?" I asked, as we bicycled slowly along. "I was looking for you."

He laughed. "I went to see Uncle Mogens. I had an idea I wanted help with."

"Oh?" I waited for an explanation, but none came. Instead, Ole scanned the street ahead, slowed his bike, and got off. "Hold this," he said, thrusting the bike at me, and when I took it he walked to where a German soldier was standing in the doorway of a store, waiting for it to open. With complete incredulity I saw Ole talk with the soldier, ask a few questions, then burst into laughter, slap the man on the back, and walk away. He took his bicycle from me, and we rode on.

"What was all *that* about?" I asked.

Ole grinned. "Look at this." He fished in his pocket, and handed me a small strip of tape. It had adhesive on the back, with a paper to keep it from sticking until the paper was peeled off. On the front were the lettered words KICK ME.

I stared at it. "You mean you just put one on that soldier?"

"That's right."

"Where'd you get it?"

"Uncle Mogens. He has whole sheets of that adhesive, so when he drops small watch parts they won't get lost on the floor. I made up a batch of labels yesterday, saying UP THE RAF, KICK ME, GERMANS GO HOME, HITLER STINKS, and so on." I started to hand it back to him, and he said, "No—keep it. See what you can do with it. It's fun."

Hesitantly, I put the label in my pocket. "What did you say while you were doing it?" I asked.

"I told him how great I thought the Volkswagens are, and wondered if he knew where I could buy one second-hand. He said I'd have to ask his commanding officer, and I asked if he thought Hitler might let me have one if I sent him a nice enough letter. He said he'd ask Hitler next time he lunched with him, and I laughed and said that was a good joke. That's all there was to it."

"I see," I said. "That's all."

"Why were you trying to find me yesterday?" Ole asked, and when I told him his eyes grew round and bright. "Hot damn!" he said. "Now we know where there's a printing press!"

"I don't think it's as easy as that," I replied. "These guys aren't likely to admit anything to a total stranger. We've got to get their confidence."

"Tell 'em what we've already done."

"Sure. Suppose they turn us in."

"Does that sound likely?"

"No, but it's possible. Or they might think we're double agents, and we'll wind up in the harbor."

"Ah, make sense. All you have to do is go back for another appointment, and very gently get across the idea that you and a friend want to help. Once you've made that move, the rest'll be easy."

"For you, maybe," I said. "I can't think as fast as you."

"Thinking has nothing to do with it! Just tell 'em the story! If I had anything wrong with my teeth *I'd* do it, but I have no reason to go there. You've got the perfect opening, so you're the one who has to do it."

"OK," I said. "I guess you're right."

So, thinking of all the things that might go wrong and hoping I didn't make a mess of it, I called the clinic, identified myself, and asked for an appointment. The dentist gave me a time to come, and, assuring my mother it was just a routine checkup, I went back to Kronprinsessegade. As I climbed the stairs I wondered what I was getting myself in for, and I suddenly realized I was excited. I felt I was on the threshold of something big, and all I hoped was I'd be able to hold up my end. People talk about turning points in their lives, but they seldom recognize them as they're happening. I think—or I like to think—that I did realize what was taking place, but if somebody asked me to swear to it, I couldn't be sure.

At any rate the dentist, who was alone in the office, sat me down and peered into my mouth with his long-handled mirror, and after a moment said, "That looks all right to me. It's coming along nicely."

"I just wanted to be sure," I said, when he'd removed the mirror.

He started to undo the bib, and I was afraid he was going to usher me out without my having been able to say a word, so I put up my hand. "The gum on the lower left-hand side feels a little sore," I said. "Do you think there's anything going on there?"

He made a quick inspection, said, "No. Perfectly healthy," and took off the bib.

All right, I thought, it's now or never. "You don't know where I could find a mimeograph machine, do you?" I said.

"No," said the dentist. "Why?"

"A friend of mine and I could use one."

"For what?" He was still holding the bib, touching the clips together.

"This and that. We were using the machine at school, but the janitor turned us in."

"Why?"

I shrugged. "He must be a Nazi."

"What's his name?"

"Emil Lund. The son of a bitch called the Gestapo."

"What did they do to you?"

"We got away. They never saw us."

"What were you doing?"

"Just mimeographing."

"What?"

I shrugged again. "A sort of news bulletin."

"About what?"

Here was the crucial point. If I told him, and he was on the wrong side, he could turn me in; if I didn't tell him, he wouldn't know where I stood. "The soccer team," I said, looking him straight in the eye.

He held my look. "What's the matter with that?"

"How do I know? Maybe the Nazis don't like soccer."

"Maybe they don't. When was this?"

"Last April. Just after the chain letters started."

"I heard about them. Did this have anything to do with that?"

"I told you, it was about the soccer team."

"That's right. I forgot."

"Well, if you hear about a machine, I'd appreciate your letting me know."

"I will."

"Thank you."

"Oh—I gather the Gestapo didn't get your names."

"No. Emil doesn't know our names. We've steered clear of him since then."

"I can see why. You say Emil Lund is his name?"

"That's right."

His eyes got a faraway look. "All right, then. I'll let you know if I hear of a mimeograph."

He ushered me out, and I left not knowing if I'd accomplished anything or not.

I told Ole about the visit, and he was disappointed. "You should have come right out with it," he said. "He wouldn't have turned you in in a million years."

"Look at it this way," I replied. "I wanted him to think I was someone who could keep a secret, so the best way was not to tell him anything. Doesn't that make sense?"

"We'll see if it does or not," said Ole.

For more than two weeks, nothing happened. The Battle of Britain reached its peak in mid-September, and everywhere you could see signs that people were rooting for the British, but in very few places could you see any hope they'd win. The only bright spot was that the BBC was as straightforward as ever, which was in a way comforting because they obviously weren't trying to hide anything, and you felt if they could still come out with the truth, then maybe everything wasn't lost after all. Hitler's theory was that if you told a big enough lie, people would believe it and all the lesser lies that followed, and although it worked for a while it was counterproductive in the end. Generally speaking, people lie only when they're in trouble, or trying to get something for nothing, and if they're telling the truth it means they're sure of their ground. I throw this in for whatever it may be worth.

After a few days of asking if I'd heard anything, Ole

gave up and adopted a reproachful attitude, as though I'd blown our one big chance to do something worthwhile. To be honest, all that the silence meant was the dentist had been unable to locate a mimeograph machine, but I think we'd both been hoping for something more. Then other subjects took precedence in our conversation, such as for instance Ingrid. One morning, when we met as usual on our way to school, Ole looked sleek and self-satisfied. We pedaled for a while before he spoke.

"Had a date last night," he said at last.

"Oh?" I said, and then, as though I didn't know, "With whom?"

"Ingrid."

Silence.

"Have a good time?"

"Yup."

Another silence.

This time Ole broke it. "We talked about you."

"Oh?"

"Uh-huh."

Long silence.

"Anything I ought to know about?"

"Probably not."

"Well, thanks for bringing it up."

"Don't mention it."

As we were dismounting in the schoolyard, he said, "She thinks you're an odd duck."

"That's nice to know," I replied. "It's good to start the day with these cheerful little tidbits."

"I just thought you might be interested," Ole said, and walked away. I was tempted to throw my books at the back of his head.

I brooded over this all day, and decided the best thing I could do would be to call her, and see if I could make a date to straighten matters out. I didn't know quite what the odd-duck remark meant—whether it was said in pique, or scorn, or amusement, or what—but I was sure it wasn't flattering. Of course, Ole might not have been reporting with total accuracy, but that was something on which only she could testify. As soon as I got home I called her, and the phone rang three times before it was picked up.

"Kaj Nielsen," came her father's voice.

"Is Ingrid there, please?" I asked.

"Who's calling?"

"Jens Hansen."

Click. Silence. Slowly, I put the instrument back in its cradle. Well, I thought. At least I know where I stand with *him*.

I ended by writing her a letter, telling of my communication problem and asking her to call me when it was feasible. I signed it "The Odd Duck." She called two days later, sounding pert and cheerful, and we made a date for the following evening. In view of her father's attitude I was to meet her at the pavilion on the Gyldenløvesgade, two blocks from her home.

The next day, I alternated between anticipation and apprehension. She'd sounded quite warm on the phone, and that was a good sign, but her remark to Ole still hovered like a vulture over the scene, and I honestly couldn't tell what to expect. As I turned into our street, a man who'd been standing on the corner came toward me. He was wearing a nondescript cloth cap and overcoat, and was someone I'd never seen before.

"Jens Hansen?" he asked, and when I nodded he said, "Come with me," and turned away.

"I can't," I said. "I've got a—an appointment."

He looked back at me. "Did you want a mimeograph machine?"

Only then did I realize what was happening. "Oh," I said. "Can I—" I wanted to get hold of Ingrid, to tell her I might be late, but I clearly couldn't call her house with the message. I couldn't think what to do. The man walked to where he'd left his bicycle, mounted it, and started to ride away. I followed.

We rode through the park behind the Art Museum, then across Kronprinsessegade and into a district of small, winding streets, the same general area where Ole's Uncle Mogens lived. As we reached the head of one street, the man said, "Go down to the last door on the left, knock twice, and then once," and with that he rode on. I veered off, went to the door he'd indicated, and left my bike against the side of the house. Feeling like a character in a motion picture, I knocked twice and then once, and waited. After a few moments the door opened, and a woman put her head out. She was middle-aged, and looked like any harried housewife. She glanced at me, then opened the door wider and said, "Come in."

"Is it all right to leave my bike outside?" I asked.

She thought for a moment, then said, "Probably better bring it in. I'm new at all this."

I brought the bike inside and left it in the front hall, and she took me back to the kitchen. Two men were sitting at the table; one was the dentist, and the other was a stranger to me.

The dentist smiled and said, "Sit down." He made no move to introduce me, so I simply nodded to the other man and sat down. I looked at the dentist, who was still smiling. "Did you think I'd forgotten you?" he asked.

"Just about," I said.

"We have to be careful."

"That's all right with me."

"Now—" He cleared his throat "—I gather you're interested in putting out news bulletins and the like. Is that correct?"

"That's correct."

"I also gather you and your friend put out that one that was a copy of the first chain letter."

"Yes, sir." I grinned with pride. "Where'd you find it?"

"On a tram."

The woman put her head through the door. "Anyone want coffee?" she asked.

"No, thank you," the other man replied.

"Tea? Hot chocolate?"

"Lise, we're busy," the man said, and she vanished.

"What's your friend's name?" the dentist asked.

"Ole Suensen," I said.

"He's Mogens Suensen's nephew, is that right?"

"That's right." I wondered what difference that made, but hesitated to ask.

"Good. Now, at the moment we're just putting out handbills—news, thoughts about sabotage, and so on—but we'd like someday to put out a regular paper. Would that sort of thing interest you?"

"Yes, sir!"

"For now, all you and Suensen can do is help distribute the handbills—get them disseminated as widely as possible. At the same time, we'd like you to develop whatever news sources you can, so that we can run a regular information bulletin."

The woman reappeared in the doorway. "Some *smørre-brød*, perhaps?" she said. "It's all ready."

"Lise!" the other man said, and she scowled at him and left.

"What kind of news sources?" I asked.

"Anything. We'll want to publish the names of Danish Nazis or collaborators. We'll want to know what firms are turning out things for the Germans. We'll want to know how various members of the Government stand on different issues. We want to *dis*courage cooperation of any sort, and *en*courage anything that'll harm the Germans."

"Speaking of that," I said, "Ole and I swiped some dynamite, but we haven't thought what to do with it yet."

The dentist gave me a long and thoughtful look. "My," he said, at last. "You are energetic, aren't you?"

"It's mostly Ole," I said. "He's the one with the ideas."

"How long have you had it?"

"Since last spring."

"Where is it?"

"In Ole's window box."

"Do you know how to use it?"

"It's not all that hard, is it?"

"It is if you do it wrong."

"Oh. I thought you just lit the fuse, and let it go."

"There's more to it than that. You ought to let an expert do it."

"Oh," I said again.

"Would you consider turning it over to us?"

"As far as I'm concerned, sure. I don't know how Ole would feel, though. We went to quite a little trouble to get it."

"Ask him, will you?"

"Sure thing."

For the first time, the other man spoke to me. "How much have you got?" he asked.

"Twelve sticks," I told him. "And a couple of coils of fuse."

"I don't need the fuse. And one stick will do for quite a while. Do you think you could get me one stick tonight?"

"What do you want just one stick for?" the dentist put in. Then, to me, "Sigvald is our explosive expert."

"Because I don't need much," Sigvald replied. "I swipe some ammo from the Germans' practice range, take one cartridge from each clip, remove the powder and fill it with dynamite, then replace the whole lot. Whoever shoots the dynamite cartridge—*blam!*—his head goes off."

"How about some Tuborg and snaps?" the woman said, coming into the room and going to the refrigerator. "I never knew a man who'd refuse Tuborg and snaps." She produced three bottles of beer and one of Aalborg akvavit, put them on the table, and gave each of us a long beer glass and a short snaps glass.

Sigvald sighed, and poured his drink. "All right," he said. "You win."

"You should never work on an empty stomach," she said, going back to the refrigerator. "It'll give you a headache." She produced a platter of smørrebrød (open-faced sandwiches) —shrimp, smoked salmon, ham, herring, and cheese—and set that in front of us. "If you need anything, just call," she said. "I'll be in the front room." And she left.

"I don't know how I keep my figure," Sigvald said, biting into a sandwich. "I guess it must be worry about my work."

"You've got a good line of work to worry about," the dentist replied.

"I tell you, Stig," said Sigvald, his mouth full, "if I spent my days with my hands in people's mouths the way you do, I'd welcome a change at the end of the day. There's nothing that gets you out of a rut like a nice, loud explosion."

"I have no complaints," the dentist said, winking at me. "I meet some interesting people in my profession."

"So do I, but I can always do with a change of pace."

"What's your real business?" I asked Sigvald.

"Obstetrics," he replied, taking another sandwich. "I'm a professor of OBS-GYN."

I thought of the movies I'd seen and the books I'd read about spies and saboteurs and the like, and I concluded that real life bears little relation to fiction. The mere fact that we were sitting here, eating and drinking while we discussed blowing people's heads off, was so unreal as to make me wonder if I was having some sort of hallucination. Then I realized that the dentist was talking to me, and I blinked and said, "I'm sorry. What did you say?"

"I said do you think you can get Sigvald his stick of dynamite tonight?"

"I don't know why not. I'll have to ask Ole."

"You can tell Ole all I've told you, but for the moment don't tell him where we are. The fewer people who know these things, the better it is all around."

"OK. But you can trust Ole with anything."

"I'm sure of that. But what he doesn't know, he can't tell if he should be—ah—put under pressure."

"Oh." I wondered how long I could hold out if I were "put under pressure," and I decided that was one of the things I'd just as soon not find out.

"All right, then," the dentist said, when we'd finished the beer and sandwiches and had one last round of snaps. "You and Sigvald go and get his dynamite, and then wait until you hear from me again."

"Do you have my phone number?" I asked.

He smiled. "Yes, but I won't use it unless I have to. You know the southern entrance to Kongens Have, at the corner of Kronprinsessegade and Gothersgade?"

"Yes," I said. Kongens Have is one of the several parks in the center of the city.

"Well, you go in that entrance, and just beyond the first path on the right there's a beech tree with a heart carved on the trunk, and the initials A.H. + B.M. The heart is really a plug, and you lift it out and there'll be a note in the cavity behind. Or there may not be. If there is, it'll just give a time, which will be the time next day you should come here. Check it daily. All right?"

"Yes," I replied. Then, out of curiosity, "What do the initials stand for?"

"Adolf Hitler and Benito Mussolini."

It was dark when Sigvald and I went out, and we walked through the shadowy streets, I wheeling my bike and he moving in slow, even strides, almost as though he were skating. His feet never seemed to leave the ground; they just glided back and forth while he steamed steadily ahead. When we reached Ole's house, I said, "I'll see if he's in," and suddenly realized Sigvald was no longer beside me. I looked around but couldn't see him, and after a moment or two I approached the front door and knocked. Ole's father answered.

"Is Ole here, Mr. Suensen?" I asked.

He stared at me. "He said he was going out with you."

Uh. Think fast. "I know. I missed him. I haven't been home since school." I started to move away.

"Any message?" Mr. Suensen asked.

"No, thank you, sir. Just tell him I'll see him tomorrow."

I made as though to walk down the street, and when Mr. Suensen closed the door I looped back, looking for Sigvald. He came out of the shadows.

"No luck?" he said.

"No, but I know where it is. Come on." We went around to the side of the house and, moving quietly, approached the window box. Sigvald stood back, to warn me if anyone came near, and I went up and dug my hands into the earth. It was loose, and as I clawed through it I came slowly to the realization that the dynamite wasn't there. I scrabbled frantically, but all I felt was the dirt beneath my fingernails and, eventually, the wooden sides and bottom of the box.

I stood back, to make sure this was where we'd put it, and there was no question. It was gone.

I reported this to Sigvald, and his face tightened and he said, "Where'd your friend go?"

"I don't know," I replied. "His father just said he was out."

"Do you think he's out to use the dynamite?"

"I don't think he'd do it without me." I tried to convince myself this was true, but I wasn't absolutely sure. Ever since my supposedly futile interview with the dentist, Ole had seemed withdrawn, almost secretive. A month ago I could have sworn he'd do nothing without me; now I couldn't.

"Do you know where he might be?"

"He could be anywhere. He might be at his Uncle Mogens'. He might—"

"Let's try there." He started off, apparently knowing exactly where Uncle Mogens lived.

"Is there some rush about getting it tonight?" I asked. "I'm sure to see him tomorrow."

"There's a rush if he's planning to use it tonight," Sigvald replied. "Unless he knows how to use it correctly, he could blow himself up."

It had never occurred to me that Ole didn't know everything; he always seemed so much in charge that he appeared to have instant knowledge at his fingertips.

We'd gone about two blocks when, far in the distance, there was a dull thud, accompanied by a flick of pressure in our ears. We looked at each other and said nothing, but Sigvald speeded up his skater's pace, and I mounted my bike to stay with him.

I don't know how long it took us to get to Uncle Mogens' house. It seemed forever, but it was probably no more than a half hour. The center of Copenhagen is so compact you can walk from one end to the other in less than an hour, and we didn't have all that far to go. When, finally, we arrived, a faint crack of light showed behind the blackout curtain, and the moment I knocked, it went out. I knocked again, and there was silence.

"Here, let me," said Sigvald, and he reached out and gave the two-one knock. After a moment we heard the sound of footsteps.

"Who's there?" came Uncle Mogens' voice, quietly.

"Sigvald," was the reply, before I could speak.

The door opened, and Uncle Mogens said, "Why didn't you—" and then he saw me, and he said, "Oh. Come in."

We went in, and through into a back room, where Ole was sitting at a red-felt-covered table with a glass of beer in front of him. He'd drunk about half of it. When he saw me, he grinned. "Greetings," he said. "I thought you had a date tonight."

I looked at my watch, and saw to my horror that it was twenty minutes to ten, and my date with Ingrid had been for seven. I stared at my watch for a few seconds, then said, "Well, I guess I don't any longer."

"There are more important things in life than women," said Ole.

"Did you know the dynamite's gone?" I asked.

"Yup. I thought it might get mushy in that wet earth."

"Where'd you put it?"

"Here and there." His eyes went to Sigvald, who was standing behind me.

"This is Sigvald—" I began, and then turned. "I'm sorry. What's your last name?"

"Sigvald will do," he replied.

"He wants to borrow a stick," I went on, then turned again. "Is it all right to tell why?"

Sigvald explained, and Ole's eyes brightened with pleasure. "For a cause like that, you can have as much as you want," he said, and stood up.

"A single stick will do for now," said Sigvald. "That's all I like to carry at one time."

"Did you hear the explosion a little while back?" I asked Ole as he left the room.

"Yup," he said.

"Do you know what it was?"

"Nope," came his voice from the other room.

"Can you make an educated guess?"

"Yup."

"What?"

He reappeared with a stick of dynamite, which he handed to Sigvald. "There's a German supply truck that suddenly disintegrated into hundreds of small pieces," he said.

I swallowed. "With the driver?"

"I wouldn't know about that. I wasn't there when it happened."

"I mean, did you wire the—"

"No. A long fuse." He stopped, glanced at Sigvald, then went on, "I gather you found other things to do."

"That's right," I said. "I'll fill you in tomorrow." Suddenly, I was limp with fatigue.

It was Sigvald's turn to look at his watch. "My God," he said, "I've got to go. I'm due at the hospital at ten." He started out.

"One of these days you're going to be late," Uncle Mogens observed.

"Haven't missed one yet," Sigvald replied, and vanished. We heard the front door quietly close behind him.

As I rode home through the darkened streets there were two things that occupied my thoughts: one, what I was going to tell my parents, and two, how I was going to square myself with Ingrid. Since neither could be achieved without lying, the problem was what lies to concoct that would stand up under the inevitable barrage of questions. If I'd been an accomplished liar it would have been one thing, but as a basically truthful soul it was a wholly different matter. So much for proper upbringing, I thought. It doesn't keep you out of trouble, and it only adds to your troubles once you're in.

Chapter Six

There was only one thing to do about Ingrid: I wrote her a letter that fairly dripped with anguish, saying if I told her the truth she wouldn't believe it, and she'd therefore have to settle for the fact that I'd been unavoidably detained. Words couldn't express how sorry I was, and I hoped she'd find it in her heart to forgive me, and so on and so on. I didn't expect it to work, and it didn't. I heard no more from her, and resigned myself to counting it one more romance gone sour. It was a painful thought, remembering the warmth and pleasure of the one date we'd had, but at the moment there wasn't much to do about it.

With my parents, it was something else again. When I got home that night my mother was on the edge of hysterics, and my father was white-faced and grim. There was so much noise when I opened the door that I don't remember any coherent words; it was just a babble of recriminations and released tension. Finally, I was able to quiet them.

"If you'll please just listen, I'll explain what happened," I said, calmly and slowly. I spoke slowly so as to be able to think what to say next; I hadn't the slightest idea what was going to follow. "In the first place, I apologize. I realize how worried you must have been, and, believe me, I wouldn't have done it if there'd been any choice."

"It's a fine time to tell us that," my mother said.

"I'm sorry, but there it is." A deep breath. *Think.* "I was on my way home from school—as a matter of fact, I was just turning into Høyensgade—when a man came up to me and asked if I was Jens Hansen." So far, wholly true. "I said I was, and he said to come with him, so I went." True. "I didn't know what he wanted; for all I knew one of you had been hurt, and he was trying to break it to me gently." Untrue. Now what? "As I say, I went with him." Pause.

"You've now said it twice," my father remarked.

"That's right. So I went with him. Then a really unbelievable thing happened. I still can't believe it." Pause.

"What?" said my father. "See if we'll believe it."

"We were in his car, and—" Beginning of an idea "—we were driving along—and suddenly another car came up, and forced us off the road. It was full of Gestapo, and they took this man and me to Shell House and questioned us for—well, until just a little while ago. It seemed like weeks."

"What did they question you about?" my father asked. "Have you been doing anything you shouldn't?"

"Me? No, *sir*. I have no idea what they wanted. All I can think is they must have had something on this other man, and they picked me up because I was with him. That's all I can think of."

"And you never found out what this man wanted of you?"

"No, sir."

"Do you know his name?"

"No, sir." Back to the truth again.

A long pause.

"And that's all?" my father said.

"That's all."

My parents looked at each other. "It's so wild I think it must have happened," my father said. "Nobody in his right mind would dream up a story like that."

"You're absolutely right," I said, relaxing. "As I said before, I can hardly believe it myself."

That winter was a cold one, in more ways than one. The Germans gave up the idea of invading England and instead consolidated their positions, getting ready, as it turned out, to invade Russia the following spring. At that time the German Army had not only been invincible; it had knocked off its adversaries with such dispatch as to make it seem pointless even to think of opposition. A good many people took the position that they'd already won, and the Danish Government's policy of collaboration seemed to be the only one that made sense.

But not everybody felt that way. Ole and I, through our news-gathering for the handbills, found out about the burgeoning of the so-called "Churchill Clubs," which were groups of students dedicated to sabotage and harassment. What they did, very simply, was anything that would raise a little hell. They stole German rifles, hand grenades, revolvers, and the like, and they sabotaged whatever targets offered themselves. The first time the Germans took official notice was when they demanded the death penalty for eight Aalborg boys who'd blown up an ammunition truck, and who had plans for an attack on a German military unit. The boys escaped the death penalty, but even if they'd been shot it wouldn't have stopped the movement; it had too much momentum. (As a matter of fact Ole and I had, without knowing it, formed an early two-man Churchill Club ourselves.)

In February of 1941, the Germans made a move that showed how little respect they really had for Danish sovereignty. They'd previously pressed for the removal of one or two unfriendly Government ministers, and the Government had complied on the reasonable ground that there was no point irritating them unnecessarily; but then, on February 5, they demanded that eight motor torpedo boats of the Danish Navy be turned over to them, and without a whimper the Government acceded. Some people were outraged, some were fatalistic, and some thought it was a smart move to keep the Germans happy, but the people who really blew their minds were the British. They were already making plans for a comeback, and while they could forgive Danish capitulation they were in no mood to overlook such blatant collaboration as this. On March 24 Rodney Gallop, of the Foreign Office, came on the BBC with a blast that was heard by the million or more Danes gathered around their radios. (The Germans tried to jam these broadcasts, but if you turned just a hair off the station it eliminated the jamming, and you could still hear fairly well.)

My parents and I were listening when Mr. Gallop started his broadcast with a quote from Hitler's *Mein Kampf*. " 'A shrewd conqueror,' " he read, " 'will always enforce his exactions on the conquered only by stages. Then he may expect that a people who have lost all strength of character, which is always the case with every nation that voluntarily submits to the threats of an opponent, will not find in any of these acts of oppression sufficient grounds for taking up arms again.' "

"You see?" my mother said, triumphantly. "What did I tell you?"

"Herta, be quiet," my father replied. "Let's hear what he has to say."

We listened, while the speaker went on to contrast the

firmness of the Danish King and people with the weakness of the Government, and then came a clear warning: "When the oppressed nations of Europe are freed, and are gathered round the table of a new peace conference, the part which will fall to each one will inevitably depend on the contribution which that country has brought to the common cause." In other words, if you're not with us now, then don't expect anything from us later on. He wound up by urging the Danish people to insist that their Government stop making concessions.

"It's all very well to talk about a peace conference," my father said, when the set had been turned off, "but what assurance do we have the British will win?"

"What assurance do we have they won't?" my mother replied.

He looked at her quietly. "They haven't done very well so far."

"They haven't been beaten," she said.

He adopted his accountant's attitude, ticking off item after item proving that the British couldn't win. "So all I'm saying," he concluded, "is that when they ask us to stand up against our Government, they're not talking from a very strong position. It's easy for them to *say*, across the Channel, but it's something else to *do*, right here."

"There are ways," my mother said.

"What do you mean?"

She suddenly looked almost prim. "You know the old saying? 'Where there's a will, there's a way.'"

"A way to do what?"

"This and that." I was reminded of Ole, when he was being elaborately casual about something.

"Herta, stop being evasive!" my father said. "What have you been doing?"

"Not much."

"But *what*?"

She touched her back hair. "Nothing, compared to some people."

All at once, my senses twanged to attention. Was she referring to me? Did she know more than I gave her credit for? I listened carefully, to see if I could detect any hint of a signal.

"You should talk to Lise Jørgensen," she went on. "Eigil's been giving her lessons in operating a drill press, so she can make parts for submachine guns."

"Mother, you shouldn't say that," I put in. "You don't want the word to get around."

She glanced at me. "I wouldn't say it outside this room. Your father may be gullible, but he's not a traitor."

"*I am not gullible!*" my father shouted. "I'm the only sensible person in this house!"

"Is that nice?" she replied. "What makes you think Jens isn't sensible?"

He subsided slowly. "I'm sorry," he said. "But gullible I am not. I just want to know what it is you've been doing."

"I told you, nothing," she said. "On the other hand, Else Bjøl says there's five times as much sabotage as we hear about. She says Danes are blowing up Danish property right and left."

"Else Bjøl would say anything, just to keep talking," my father replied. "As nature abhors a vacuum, so Else Bjøl abhors a silence."

"That's as may be. It doesn't mean she's always wrong."

"Let's get back to you. You said you've been doing nothing compared to some people. That implies you've been doing something. What is it?"

"It's none of your business."

"It certainly is my business! If the Gestapo are going to be coming to my house, I want to know what they're coming for!"

"You won't be seeing the Gestapo, I promise. Now just simmer down, and forget I spoke. I was only teasing."

He glared at her for a few moments, then said, "If it *was* teasing, I do not consider it funny."

"I'm sorry," she replied. "Next time, I'll try for a few laughs." And with that she got up and left the room, leaving me awash with admiration. This was a side of her I'd never seen before, and all I could think was the stage had missed a great actress when she got married.

It's strange how some things seem to happen spontaneously, and how a whole city will react in a certain way with little advance notice or preparation. Take, for instance, the Wednesday in April when I'd ducked out of school before the lunch hour, to check the tree in Kongens Have for messages. I was crossing Town Hall Square when the clock began to chime noon, and suddenly everything went still. Only the chimes continued, and when they stopped I realized that the whole city had stopped; trams, buses, bicyclists, pedestrians were absolutely motionless. People were standing at attention, and as I got quietly off my bike I noticed some of them were wearing black neckties. Only then I realized it was April 9, the anniversary of the invasion. I stood at attention, with the backs of my eyes stinging, and for two minutes nothing moved. Two German soldiers, coming down Strøget, froze like statues when they saw everyone else, although they probably had no idea what it was all about. At the end of the two minutes everyone and everything started again, like a film being run through a projector. I blew my nose, got back on my bike, and rode to Kongens Have.

A couple of other things happened that spring that are worthy of mention. Of course, the big thing was the German invasion of Russia, but I'm talking about events that had an immediate impact on us in Denmark, and gave a hint of the shape of the future. The most important was the appearance of *De Frie Danske,* the first underground newspaper to be published. It had a flag on its banner line on page 1 and news of the forced resignation of Christmas Møller from Parliament, as well as the news of the formation of the Danish Council in London, which had been successfully jammed by the Germans when it was broadcast on the BBC; and a blacklist of names and addresses of Danes sympathetic to the Germans. The reaction of our group, who were still hoping to put out a regular paper, was one of mixed envy and applause. We wondered if there wasn't some way to join forces with them, since we had better printing facilities (their first issue was done on a typewriter) and they clearly had the news sources. By discreet investigation, through our own sources, we found it was published by ten men known as the Valby Group, named after the suburb of Copenhagen where they met, and that students at Copenhagen University, especially medical students, were involved in the work. We got word to the Valby Group, and they declined our offer of cooperation —which was one of the luckiest things that could have happened to us. Within eighteen months the leaders were arrested, and subsequently tried and sent to jail. There'll be more about their arrest later on.

De Frie Danske was a powerful force. It appeared fortnightly and reported, sometimes on the same day they happened, secret Foreign Office meetings, Cabinet meetings, and the like, and its circulation jumped from two thousand the first issue to five thousand, and its size to sixteen pages, with an estimated fifty thousand readers. It was distributed partly by post and partly during the blackout, and a copy of each issue managed to reach the King in Amalienborg. It drove the Germans crazy.

Another event was the arrival of the "V" campaign in Denmark. In January, the BBC had initiated a campaign in

Belgium, whereby people scrawled a V for *Victoire* on walls, sidewalks, and wherever they could, simply as a sign of resistance and as an irritant to the Germans. It could be done quickly and with almost no danger, and it caught on fast. The V also stood for *Vrijheid,* or freedom, in Flemish, and while the Danish equivalents of victory and freedom did not begin with a V, a way was found to use it by the phrase *Vi Vil Vinde!* ("We Will Win!"), which was the same in Norwegian. The V slogan spread throughout occupied Europe; it was translated into sound by taking the dot-dot-dot-dash of the Morse code V, and emphasizing it in the opening bars of Beethoven's Fifth Symphony. The *boom-boom-boom BOOM* was used on BBC programs and in concert halls; it was a rallying sign for all the subjugated people, and Churchill was usually photographed making the V sign with his fingers. Lamely, the Germans tried to say it stood for the German work *Viktoria,* but nobody even bothered to laugh. "Vi Vil Vinde" was scratched in the dirt on a road in Norway, photographed from the air, and used on a stamp issued by the Norwegian Government-in-exile in London. Seen in perspective it was a small thing, but when people have little to hope for, then even the smallest things can become important.

But the thing that showed the true temper of the Danish people, and foreshadowed the trouble that was to come, was what happened on Thursday, June 5, Danish Constitution Day. It was a holiday, and Ole and I had no school; we were about to graduate anyway, and most of our work was done. We decided to go to the Denmark-Sweden football match, which was an annual event and always hard-fought. The Danes and Swedes are great rivals in this respect.

Danish, Swedish, and Nazi flags were flying over the Stadion as we mingled with the crowd funneling toward the entrance gates. There were a lot of police in their white-topped caps, but the mood of the crowd was generally jovial, and it didn't seem likely police would be necessary. The beer and hot-dog vendors were doing a brisk business, and everyone was looking forward to a good, bruising game. But when we got inside the Stadion, there was a subtle change of atmosphere. Nazi banners were everywhere; the black Swastika in its white circle on the blood-red field seemed to leer at us from all directions. A Nazi band was thumping out martial music, there was a great deal of stiff-arm saluting and *Heil Hitler*ing, and all at once the beer and hot dogs tasted sour and the mood changed from expectation to simmering rage.

Then came the national anthems, and after the Danish and Swedish anthems had been sung, the crowd, just as though they'd rehearsed it, went on and sang the Norwegian anthem as a slap at the Germans.

In the stands near us were four German soldiers, their uniforms immaculate and their mouths full of hot dogs, and they were talking in that Teutonic tone of voice that makes every sentence a flat statement. I couldn't hear what they said, but I saw a Dane in the row ahead of them turn around and glare. His face was red and his eyes were bright, and suddenly he reached out and shoved one of the Germans. A scuffle developed; the other soldiers joined in, and then people were on them from all sides, punching, kicking, and wielding bottles. All over the Stadion people suddenly turned on the Germans; all their pent-up emotion overflowed, and bottles began to fly through the air. Those who were near the Germans tried to get at them; those farther away threw bottles in their general direction, and in no time at all the entire Stadion was a mass of fighting, shouting people, with bottles soaring like sea gulls. The police swarmed in, blowing their whistles and wielding their clubs, and by the time order was finally restored several score people had been arrested. It was the last international football game during the Occupation.

So much for peaceful coexistence between Aryan Nordic cousins; it became progressively easier for a Dane to be arrested. Putting out a cigarette on a German poster, addressing a German soldier in English, spreading malicious gossip, and other such heinous crimes meant automatic jail sentences if the offenders were caught. (Later on, when the Germans became more jittery, it became dangerous even to look at them; one soldier jumped out of a marching column and bayoneted a twelve-year-old boy who'd smiled at them as they passed.)

The main effect of the German invasion of Russia, as far as Denmark was concerned, was that after June 22 the Danish Communists went underground. Many were arrested and sent to Horserød prison camp and later to German K-2 camps, and the remainder joined actively in the Resistance. This was a decided advantage for the Danes, because until then the Communists had been pretending they were friendly with the Germans, and now their considerable skill at organizing underground activities was put to work for us. They were the only Danes who'd actively trained at sabotage and subterranean work, and they were invaluable. Aksel Larsen, chairman of the Danish Communist Party and a member of Parliament, lived on the loose, staying with friends who had good chimneys, trapdoors, haystacks, and other handy hiding places, and he was instrumental in putting out two more underground papers, *Land og Folk* (*Land and People*) and the more ponderously titled *Politisk Maanedsbrev* (*Monthly Political Letter*).

After the football fiasco, there wasn't another really good riot until the fall. The cause of this one was political, and before describing it I should explain that Dr. Munch, the nice old pacifist Foreign Minister, had been succeeded in July of 1940 by Erik Scavenius, an anti-British, pro-German aristocrat. He disliked the Danish Nazis, but that was about all that could be said for him. During the summer of 1941, when the Germans were apparently making short work of the Russian Army, Scavenius was summoned to Berlin to discuss signing the Anti-Comintern Pact, an anti-Communist document drawn up by Germany, Italy, Japan, and the other Axis powers. On November 25 he signed it, thereby making Denmark as good as an ally of the Axis, and when the word reached Copenhagen all hell broke loose.

Ole and I were enrolled in the University, and although the news wasn't received there first, it was the first place to react. Students are traditionally hair-trigger where matters of national policy are concerned—some cynics maintain it's simply a device to keep from going to classes—and at about two PM, shortly after we heard about the signing, a group of us decided to go down to Amalienborg castle, and show our displeasure. (And here is the illogic of the whole thing: the King would have been the last man in the world to approve the signing, yet we felt we had to demonstrate in front of his palace.) A theological student named Jørgen Gudme drew up a resolution condemning Scavenius, the Germans, the Anti-Comintern Pact, and life in general, and off we went. It was a cold, raw day; it had been raining and the streets were wet, but by the time we reached Amalienborg we were several hundred strong, and noisy. The hastily called police tried to herd us in, and their job was made more difficult by the fact that people came down every side street to join us, and the crowd became as uncontainable as a thunderstorm.

Jørgen Gudme stood on a wall and tried to read his resolution, which was a mistake on at least two counts: One, nobody could hear him, and two, it gave the police a focal point for their action, and they rushed in and collared him and took him away. Then they turned their attention to the rest of us, and just as they were getting nasty someone had the inspiration of singing the National Anthem. We all chimed in, singing at the top of our voices, and the police had to relax. Legally speaking, we had every right in the world to sing the National Anthem in front of the King's palace, and they'd only make fools of themselves if they tried to arrest us.

Then, ten abreast, we marched to a much more logical place—the office of the Danish Nazi paper *Fædrelandet*. The police followed along, nipping at our flanks like wolves around a herd of caribou, but by now we numbered several thousand, and all they could do was make sporadic charges, from which the people fled momentarily and then re-formed elsewhere. After letting the staff at *Fædrelandet* know how we felt, we moved off to the Parliament House and the Foreign Office, singing and shouting and waving flags. Don't ask me where the flags came from; we didn't have any when we started, but by the time the evening was over we looked like a regular parade, with flags of Denmark, Norway, Sweden, Finland, and even Iceland. We sang "Ja vi elsker" (the Norwegian national anthem), we sang every patriotic song we could think of, and we chanted "Down with Scavenius!" and "Down with the traitors!" until I was almost as hoarse as I'd been on the King's birthday.

Then, when darkness had fallen and we'd run out of other places to go, we headed for the German headquarters in the d'Angleterre. Here the police made a determined stand, which was probably just as well. They'd been reinforced by batteries of searchlights, and they attacked us with truncheons and fired blank shots from their pistols, and it soon became apparent we weren't going to get close to the d'Angleterre without some serious casualties. We veered off and milled through the streets, breaking windows in German or Nazi property, and in general behaving like a lot of hoodlums. In all such disturbances there's usually at least one funny thing that happens, and in this case it was the German who, thinking this was an anti-Comintern demonstration, came out on a balcony and gave the Nazi salute. He stood there, arm stiffly outstretched, and then someone picked up a bun of horse manure (which was plentiful because of the gas rationing) and flung it at the balcony. It rose in an arc, shedding a fine comet tail of oats, and disintegrated against the side of the building. Others with better aim flung more of the same missiles, and in short order the German scuttled back inside, frantically brushing his clothes.

Next day, the only mention of the affair in the Copenhagen papers was a note saying that tram service had been briefly interrupted in several places.

As a side note, it was during that riot that someone realized the Icelandic national anthem, "Eldgamla Isafold," had the same tune as "God Save the King." Thus one could whistle it in the presence of Germans with impunity, because when they called you on it (all English or anti-German songs were banned) you said it was in protest against the British occupation of Iceland. There was nothing they could do.

Not quite two weeks later the United States base at Pearl Harbor was attacked by the Japanese, and on December 11, Germany and Italy declared war on the United States. This was heartening news because it meant that one more ally had been added to our side, and while nobody had yet beaten the Germans, the more they tipped the odds against themselves the better it was for us. It would be hard to say we saw light at the end of the tunnel, but at least things weren't as black as they had been.

Then, at the end of the year, came another glimmer of hope. Eight British parachutists were dropped into Denmark, intending to set up contact with our scattered, largely inefficient underground. Six of them were, unhappily, caught, but it meant that the British had finally taken the initiative. They were still fighting for their lives, and it would be more than a year before they could supply us with any meaningful help, but at least they were trying. So, for everybody except the six parachutists, December 27 was the best day we'd known in quite a while.

Chapter Seven

During most of this time, Ole and I had been doing work that we considered useful, but dull. We took bundles of handbills, disguised as laundry, and distributed them throughout the city; we gathered news from whatever sources we could find; and, on request from the dentist—whom I still knew only as Stig—we got to work compiling data on the backgrounds of the Danish Nazis for publication. *That* part of the work was fascinating; it turned out that about eighty per cent of those people had records of either criminal or moral offenses; they were the real muck from the bottom of the barrel, who'd joined the Party because it gave them a chance to strut about and look important.

Then, in April of 1942, a new underground paper appeared; it was called *Frit Danmark*, and it was put out by John Christmas Møller, the Conservative Minister the Germans had forced out of office, and Aksel Larsen, head of the by-now-illegal Communist Party. In the interest of national unity Møller and Larsen formed the United Danish Front, but the heat became too great for Møller and in May he fled to England, where he broadcast for the BBC and spent the rest of the war working for the Danish cause.

But with the appearance of *Frit Danmark*, Ole felt that the information field was becoming overcrowded. (Little did he know; by the end of the war there would be about 180 underground papers.)

"What we need is a change," he said one evening, when we'd finished with our handbills. "Our talents aren't being put to their fullest use."

"Oh?" I said, guardedly. "Any ideas?"

"Yes." (I should have known better than to ask.) He looked at the sky for a moment, then said, "Ever think of going in the motion picture business?"

"You mean as an actor?' It had been my pain that I considered myself too gawky to be good-looking, but I'd always had a sneaking desire to act.

"No," said Ole, disgustedly. "As an exhibitor."

"What are you talking about?"

"You know that German film *Sieg im Westen*?"

"I've heard of it." It was a documentary on the German victories leading to the fall of France; its title meant "Victory in the West."

"They're showing it in Hellerup."

"So?"

"So wouldn't it be nice if we could louse it up?"

"How?"

"Take it off, and put on a Mickey Mouse."

"Ole, you're crazy. How could we do a thing like that?"

"Simple. Tie up the projectionist, then—"

"How? Ask him to lie down?"

"Put a gun on him."

"You got a gun?"

"I've got a couple."

I felt the familiar cold spot in my stomach. "Where'd you get them?"

"You guess."

"You mean your Uncle Mogens makes guns *too*?"

"No, but he has contacts. Some are being run across from Sweden, and some are . . ." He let the sentence trail off.

"Some are what?"

"Some are—well, sort of homemade. The RAF has been dropping instructions."

"For what?"

"For making—well, nine-millimeter pistols, Mark II Sten guns, hand grenades—you name it."

"And I'm supposed to shoot a gun that was made in someone's basement?"

"You're not supposed to shoot it, ninny. You just hold it on the man."

"And if he objects?"

Ole shrugged. "Those are the breaks of the game."

I tried to think of something to say. The whole thing sounded insane, but Ole was treating it as though we were going to a regular movie. "Do you have a film to put in its place?" I asked.

"That's the one hitch. I'm working on that now."

I felt slightly more relaxed. "Mickey Mouse can't be too easy to get these days," I said.

"I'm not holding out for Mickey Mouse," said Ole. "I'll take anything that'll serve the purpose."

Two days later, when I met him, his face was one broad, toothy smile. "I've got it," he said. "We're on for tonight."

I tried to think of a way out, but couldn't. "Is it a Mickey Mouse?" I asked.

"No." His smile became even wider.

"What is it?"

"You'll see."

"Where'd you get it?"

"Your friend Sigvald got it for me."

I thought of Sigvald the explosives expert, and wondered what kind of film he'd be using, then decided not to worry about it. The most important thing was not the film, but what we were going to do with it.

Hellerup is an area in the northern part of the city, near the Tuborg breweries, and to get there we took a tram. Ole brought with him a small bag, such as athletes use for carrying their gear, and he completed the impression by wearing sneakers. We both wore caps, which turned out to be the luckiest move of the evening. My mouth was as dry as before a football game, and I had trouble convincing myself of what we were doing.

The film had already started when we reached the theater. Ole went to the box office while I stood behind him, trying not to look as though I was about to throw up. I heard the girl ask him if we had reservations, and when he said no she said she could only give us balcony seats.

"That's fine," he replied, and put his money through the window.

We went up to the balcony and then, with the thunder of the German invasion forces ringing in our ears, we found the small staircase to the projection room. Halfway up, Ole opened his bag, reached in, and handed me a crude-looking machine pistol, with the grip bound in black tire tape. It was a good thing it was sticky, because my hand was so wet with perspiration I'd have dropped it otherwise. "Shouldn't we cover our faces?" I whispered, wiping my other hand on my trousers.

Ole shook his head, produced a pistol for himself, then crept up the stairs. At the top he paused in front of the door, tested the knob, then pushed it open and pointed his gun inside.

The projectionist was sitting with his chair tipped back against the wall, reading a magazine. The only sound in the booth was the whirring of the projector, which looked as big as a howitzer, and when the projectionist saw us his eyes widened, and he let his chair come slowly to the floor.

"What do *you* want?" he asked.

"Nothing much," Ole replied. "Just lie down, and take it easy."

"What are you going to do?" The projectionist sounded more curious than afraid.

"First, we're going to tie you up," Ole said, producing some rope from the bag. "Then we're going to make a little change in the program here." He brought out a can of film and laid it on the floor.

"Hell, you don't have to tie me up for that," the projectionist said. "I'm so sick of this bloody film I could scream."

Ole hesitated, then said, "It'll look better for you if we tie you. You don't want the boys thinking you helped us, do you?"

"I guess not," said the projectionist. He lay on the floor, put his hands behind his back, and rolled on one side. "Try not to tie me too tight," he said, as Ole got to work. "My circulation isn't all it used to be."

"I don't think you'll be alone for long," Ole replied. "Something tells me you'll have company very shortly." He tied the man's hands and feet, then stood up and approached the projector.

"You know how that thing works?" the projectionist asked, from the floor.

"I know how this *sort* of thing works," said Ole. "I've never seen one quite like this."

"OK. To take the cover off, you push that button on the

left." Ole did as directed and the cover came off, exposing the spinning reels of film. Then, following the instructions of the projectionist, he cut the German film, stopped the machine, and began to thread our substitute into place. A buzzer rang on the wall telephone. Then it rang again.

"What'll I say?" I asked, going to the phone.

"Better give it to me," said the projectionist. The cord was long enough so I could place the instrument against his head, and he spoke into it. "I *told* you you needed a new print," he said. "I'm trying to splice it now, but I don't know how long it'll hold." Then he nodded to me, and I hung it back on the wall. "I'll say you put a gun at my head," he told me. "They'll never know the difference."

By this time Ole had finished his end of the work, and he clapped the cover in place. Then he looked at the projectionist. "I want to thank you, friend," he said. "We'd never have done it without you."

"My pleasure," the projectionist replied. "It's the first interesting evening I've had in years."

Ole turned to me. "Now," he said, reaching for the projector switch, "you and I are going to have to get out of here— fast." He flipped the switch and ran for the door, with me behind him. As we pounded down the stairs to the balcony and then to the main floor I tried to see what the film was, but I couldn't. All I could hear was an odd reaction beginning to spread through the audience, and then we were through the doors and at the box office, and as good as away.

"Wait a minute," Ole said, and I stopped in midflight to see him go to the box office, point his pistol at the girl, and say something. She began to riffle through drawers, dropping papers in her fright, and he gestured at her with his pistol.

"Ole!" I screamed. "Come on!"

"Come back here!" he replied. "Cover the doors behind me!"

I pointed my pistol at the theater doors, just as they burst open and revealed the tall, black-uniformed figure of SS Officer Schlemmer, the man who'd caught us writing on the d'Angleterre.

"Don't move!" I shrieked at him, at the same time pulling my cap low and covering my face with one hand. "Don't move or I'll shoot!" He'd started to reach for his gun, but his hand stopped halfway to the holster.

"OK," said Ole, behind me. "Let's go!" He fired a shot into the floor at Schlemmer's feet and the SS man tumbled back into the theater, then Ole and I raced out into the night. As we went down a side street we heard shouts and one pistol shot, and then we left everything behind, and all we heard were our pounding feet and gasping breaths. We ran all the way to the Tuborg breweries, where there's a small boat basin, and where in a final emergency we could hide in the water. When at last we felt safe, we sank to the ground and gulped in the cool night air. The smell of the water was refreshing, and after about five minutes I was able to speak.

"What did you stop for?" I asked. "What in the hell was all *that* important?"

"Ho, ho," said Ole, and spat.

"Ho ho what?"

"When that girl asked if we had reservations, it gave me an idea. So as we left I asked for her list of people who reserve seats, and that's what I've got. It ought to make interesting reading."

I lay back. "It almost made *us* interesting reading," I said.

"Almost isn't good enough," said Ole.

"Is it all right to tell me now what that film was?"

He laughed. "Sigvald got it at the hospital. It's a training film on obstetrics."

"What's Ingrid's father's name?" Ole asked next day.

I thought for a moment. "Kaj."

"Ho."

"Why?"

"He's on that list."

I thought some more. "I guess that figures."

"Is he a Nazi?"

"I don't know. Maybe, maybe not."

"Is she?"

"You ought to know better than that," I said. "Of course not. Didn't you see her RAF beret?"

"That doesn't prove anything."

"Well, to me it does." I was irritated, without knowing exactly why. "That, and a lot of other things. She is not a a Nazi."

Ole shrugged. "No offense. I was only asking."

"It was still a stupid question."

He looked at me with mild amusement. "For someone who hasn't seen her in—what? A year?—you're awfully protective."

"Nothing of the sort. I just said it was a stupid question."

"Have it your way. Do you think we should publish his name?"

I thought for a second. "I don't know why not. She wouldn't mind, and it might do the old bastard good."

"All right. We'll see what happens."

"Speaking of Nazis," I said, "what about Emil? Shouldn't he be on a list of some sort?"

"Emil who?" said Ole.

"Lund. The janitor at school."

"Hadn't you heard? He had an accident."

"When?"

"A while back. He was run over."

"Killed?"

"Uh-huh."

I thought back to the expression on the dentist's face when

I told him of Emil's turning us in to the Gestapo, and I felt odd in my stomach. "What hit him?" I asked.

"Apparently hit-and-run. He was just found in the street."

I ran the tip of my tongue over my lips. "Well, well," I said, and let it go at that.

"I tell you, there's one more name we should look into," Ole said. "That's our chum Holger Andersen. He'd be a natural for the *Frikorps*."

I should explain that our interest in the local Nazis at this time was prompted by the fact that the Germans had organized what they called the *Frikorps Danmark*, or Danish Free Corps, composed of volunteers to fight the Russians on the Eastern Front. They were doing some high-power recruiting for the Frikorps, and at the same time we were trying to show the Nazis up for what they were. Holger Andersen, I reflected, would be one of the better-class Frikorps members; he was our old Boy Scout patrol leader whom we'd seen the day of the invasion, and except for his starry-eyed enthusiasm for the Germans there was nothing serious to be said against him. I remembered how his mother used to provide him with food for our hikes, and I wondered how he'd do out in the field without his mother to cater to him, and I concluded that his gung ho attitude would probably see him through. Holger was spoiled, and probably weak, but that still left him a sterling character compared to some of the others. Christmas Møller, in an article in *Frit Danmark*, had called on everyone to fight the Germans and the Danish Nazis as "our enemies by nature," and I guess that summed it up about as well as anything.

"I haven't seen Holger since that day," I said to Ole. "Do you think he enlisted right away?"

"I wouldn't be surprised," he replied. "At any rate, it wouldn't hurt to check."

The importance of knowing who stood where was best illustrated by the way in which the Germans finally managed to catch the *Frie Danske* people. Since the appearance of the first issue they'd been trying to identify the writers, and to this end they recruited two Danish Nazis to study the various prose styles in the paper, mingle with groups who might be involved, and try to identify the writers by their styles. It didn't work for a number of reasons, among them the fact that the *Frie Danske* staff got wind of it, assigned some people to read the writings of the two Nazis, then copied *their* styles in the paper, thereby leaving them chasing their own tails. The Germans finally gave up and handed the job over to the Danish police, who needless to say couldn't cut it either.

Then, in the summer of 1942, word got around that a highly-placed Dane had offered 25,000 kroner to the paper, and would send an intermediary to discuss details with the staff. They met at a specified restaurant, and shortly thereafter the whole editorial board was arrested. It turned out that the intermediary was one Carlis Hansen, who'd left Denmark after a scandal in 1936 and had joined the Gestapo. Pictures taken at the meeting identified the board, and that was that. Their trial lasted six months, and in all, thirty-two men were sentenced to terms ranging from eighteen months to ten years, and three of them were transported to Germany.

So much for talking to strangers.

In that same summer, organized sabotage began to blossom all over. The reasons for this are obscure; the British weren't yet in a position to give any substantial help, and the BBC was playing down the idea of random sabotage, so I guess it was that the Danes were finally beginning to feel they'd had enough. The idea of benign coexistence had long since soured with many people, but the Government still plodded along that course, so a feeling of real frustration developed. And when people are frustrated for long enough, they tend to want to hear things go *boom*.

One day when I checked the tree in Kongens Have, I got a different kind of note. Instead of giving me a time to be at Sigvald's house, it said, "You need an inlay," and after a little thought I concluded it meant for me to check the clinic. I did, and the dentist gave me a time to be there. A patient was in the chair when I arrived, and another came in while I was waiting, so I could see this was a regular business day, and we wouldn't be able to do much talking. When, finally, he called me in, he slipped a note in the pocket of my jacket as I sat in the chair, then clipped the bib around my neck.

"Open wide," he said, putting the mirror in my mouth.

"I heel hine," I replied. "Hus hiss aout?"

He took the mirror out of my mouth. "Rinse." he said. I rinsed, and whispered, "Why here?"

"Variety," he replied, turning the suction pipe up to a loud gurgle. "Variety is the spice of life."

I realized I wasn't going to get anything from him now, so I sat back and let him fool around in my mouth, neatening and cleaning and tidying. Then, in a low voice, he said, "Good luck," and took off the bib, in a louder voice adding, "That ought to hold you for a while." I thanked him, and went out. There were two people in the waiting room as I left, and for their benefit I tried to look like someone who'd been through great pain.

When I got outside, I took the note from my pocket and read it. It directed that Ole and I be in front of the Botanical Museum on Gothersgade at eight thirty that evening, and that was all. I should perhaps point out that, since I was now enrolled in the University, my parents didn't keep as strict an eye on my hours as they had previously. I tried to keep my mother thinking I was going out with a particular girl, but she seemed not as interested as before, and the pretense was unnecessary. Maybe she thought I was studying at the University—I don't know. All I do know is it was a relief not to be questioned all the time.

Ole and I got to the Botanical Museum early, then walked on down Gothersgade, timing ourselves so we could turn around and be back in front of the Museum at exactly eight-thirty, thus avoiding the impression of loitering. We were back on the minute, just as a woodburning car drove up to the curb, and it slowed down long enough for us to get in, then sped off. We didn't know the driver, but I recognized Sigvald sitting up next to him. The car seemed to sound different, and have more power than the usual woodburners, and I looked at Sigvald for an explanation. (Technical note: Burning wood, coal, or charcoal gives off a flammable gas which, piped into the engine of an automobile, will make a fair substitute for gasoline. The burner is towed behind the car on a dolly-like trailer.)

"You like our engine?" Sigvald asked.

"I do indeed," I replied. "I'd almost think you were using gasoline."

"Don't tell anyone, but we are," said Sigvald. "There's a faulty lock on one of the Germans' gas pumps." As an afterthought he added, "It's faulty now; it wasn't until recently."

"Is it all right to ask where we're going?" I said.

"Of course," said Sigvald. "The Blønders Shoe Factory."

"Why?"

"They're making boots for the Germans."

I thought for a moment. "How do you blow up a lot of boots?"

"You don't. You burn 'em."

"That'll take some fire, won't it?"

"That's just what we're going to give them."

I was on the point of asking how, then decided I'd find out soon enough.

We drove in silence for a while, then Sigvald said, "I don't suppose either of you boys has ever seen a Caesarian section." Ole and I admitted we hadn't, and he went on, "I did one about an hour ago, and I must say it made me think. When I lifted this fetus-turned-infant out into the air I wondered what I was letting it in for, and I was half tempted to see if I couldn't sew it back into the womb. You take a lot of responsibility on yourself when you bring a child into the world these days."

"It was hardly your fault it was being born," Ole observed.

"That's what I told myself. But if there'd been some dresser drawer where I could have stashed it, or some back burner to put it on until all this was over, believe me I'd have done it. The whole world is in a mess, and it's going to get a lot worse before it's better."

"Who do you think's going to win?" I asked.

Sigvald gave me a look as though I'd just belched at the dinner table. "We are, of course," he said. "It may take a while, and a lot of people may get hurt, but we've got more going for us than they do. You can't subjugate the whole world, and expect to keep it down for long."

The car pulled into a parking lot and stopped beside a long, two-story building. Sigvald glanced at it and said, "That's going to take a lot of wax. I hope we brought enough."

"*Wax?*" I said, thinking I hadn't heard right.

"Paraffin," he replied, getting out of the car. "One of the best igniters there is." We went around to the woodburner, opened the side, and there were four buckets of paraffin, warming on the coals. "We make a trail out of this throughout the whole place," he said, and lifted out the buckets.

The driver had in the meantime been working on the door to the building, and as we approached with the paraffin he got it open. As we went in, he said, "The guard was last here a half hour ago. That gives us about an hour."

"Good," said Sigvald. "We'll need it. Get the other stuff, will you?"

The driver disappeared, and returned with four flashlights and a lot of other items I couldn't identify. Each of us took a bucket of wax and a flashlight, and, working carefully so as not to get too much in any one spot, we made a solid line of paraffin on the floor along one wall. The place smelled strongly of leather and oil, and I hated to think what the stench would be like when it started to burn. When we'd used up the wax, Sigvald unrolled a large ball of twine to act as a wick, and then, at various spots along the trail, he put piles of rags that smelled of kerosene. The driver was, in the meantime, doing something at the far end of the building. I shone the flashlight on my watch, and saw we'd used up half an hour.

"All right," Sigvald said, at last. "Let's go."

He made one final pile of rags near the door, and when we were all ready he lit a match, and touched it to a rag. There was a flare of fire which, at first slowly as lava then with increasing speed, spread along the trail of wax. Sigvald slammed the door, and we hurried to the car.

As we sped down the street, Sigvald glanced once behind us to see if we were being followed, and then settled back in his seat. "Where'd you plant it?" he asked the driver.

"By the center beam," the driver replied. "It ought to bring the whole second floor down."

"That'll make a merry blaze," said Sigvald. Then he laughed and turned to us. "Those British kill me," he said. "Did you see the leaflets they dropped on the German invasion troops?"

"Invasion of what?" I asked.

"When they were going to invade England. The story is the British were ready to meet them with burning oil, if they ever made the crossing. Anyway, the RAF dropped leaflets on their staging area, and one of them was a handy phrase book for German tourists in England. It was just beautiful. My personal favorite was *"Merken Sie, wie lebhaft brennt unser Kapitän."* "

I laughed, and Ole said, "What's it mean?"

" 'See how briskly our Captain burns,' " said Sigvald, his voice cracking with joy.

"Jesus! Behind us!" said the driver, and as the car lurched in a burst of speed we turned and looked, and there, apparently out of nowhere, came the unmistakable lights of a Mercedes. The driver put on all the speed he could, but the other car gained fast, and it soon pulled alongside and edged us toward the curb. We slowed to a stop, and my heart was pounding so hard I could feel it in my eardrums. My mouth was dry as sandpaper, and I wondered if either Sigvald or the driver had a gun. Neither Ole nor I had brought one, and I resolved never again to go out unarmed. It was one of those resolutions one usually makes when it's much too late, and it was of no help at the moment.

As we came to a stop, Sigvald turned to Ole and me. "You're sick!" he hissed. "Both of you! Stomach cramps! Nausea! Vomiting! Groaning! Get with it!"

Two burly men in trenchcoats got out of the Mercedes and came toward the driver's window. One carried a flashlight and the other a gun. Ole and I began to groan as the one with the flashlight said, in bad Danish, "Where do you think you're going?"

"Officer, I'm a doctor," Sigvald said. "I've got to get these men to the hospital."

Ole and I groaned louder, and began to thrash about.

"Let's see your papers," the Gestapo man said, and while Sigvald reached for his wallet I made loud retching noises and Ole gave a fair imitation of a pig stuck under a gate.

"They've got food poisoning," Sigvald said, handing his papers across. "If I don't get their stomachs pumped out, they may die."

"Angels and ministers of grace defend us!" shrieked Ole, who was taking a course in *Hamlet*, and with that he threw up on the floor.

The Gestapo man examined Sigvald's papers with his flashlight, and it took him so long I thought he was memorizing them. Then he handed them back. "What about you?" he said, to the driver.

"I don't feel so good myself," the driver said.

"Let's see your papers."

"O what a rogue and peasant slave am I!" groaned Ole, with a few more revolting noises. I was afraid he was going to overdo it, but the Gestapo man's Danish wasn't good enough to catch the translation—and even if he had, he probably wouldn't have recognized the source. I had a sudden wild desire to laugh.

Before the driver could produce his papers, Sigvald said, "Officer, are you prepared to take the responsibility if these men die? I'm telling you, as a doctor, they need immediate hospitalization."

"All in good time." The Gestapo man took the driver's papers.

"Give me your name!" Sigvald said, in a drill-sergeant's voice.

"Kemmerich. Klaus Kemmerich," the Gestapo man replied, instinctively obeying the command. Then he quickly handed the papers back. "All right, Doc, get going," he said.

We drove off, all of us feeling slightly limp, and Sigvald turned and gave Ole a baleful look. "I didn't mean you to go *that* far," he said.

"I'm sorry," Ole replied, ineffectively mopping the floor with his handerchief. "I didn't intend to. But I suddenly recognized him."

"From where?"

"He was one of those who came to the school when Emil turned us in."

Sigvald was silent for a moment. "Well, now you know his name," he said.

"The one I was worried about was the other one," the driver said. "He was snooping around behind the car."

"So?" said Sigvald.

"The dumb clot didn't realize our burner isn't going. If they'd known we're using real gas, we'd have had it."

This time the silence lasted for several minutes. I had opened my mouth to say something, when there came that familiar dull thud in the distance. Sigvald looked at his watch, and then at the driver.

"Nice timing," he said.

Considering the fact that we were using makeshift equipment, a remarkable amount of sabotage was accomplished that summer. It finally reached the point where Prime Minister Buhl became nervous and warned that the Germans might use it as a pretext to take over the Government, but the difference between the collaborationists running it and the Germans running it was so slight that the warning had little effect. What the Germans did was much more clever: They hired Danes as armed guards in factories that were likely to be sabotaged, thus setting up the situation where Danes would be shooting at Danes. The employment situation was such that they could always find people willing to work, even particularly dirty work like this. But the sabotage continued, and there was a good deal of street fighting with the Danish Nazis; and signs began to appear in stores saying "Germans not wanted here." (One store had a sign, "We prefer to do business with Germans," and passersby were irritated until they realized it was a coffin maker's.)

What brought matters to a head was something so slight that under other circumstances it would probably have been shrugged off, but as it was the repercussions were sharp and far-reaching. In September, on the King's seventy-second birthday, Hitler sent him a telegram that was fulsome, flowery, and flattering, and the King snapped back the reply: "Thanks. Christian X." Hitler was wild. He'd been insulted. He demanded thirty thousand Danish volunteers to fight in Russia; he brought back elements of the Frikorps to act as storm troops and street fighters in their own country; he replaced von Renthe-Fink, his Minister in Copenhagen, with Werner Best, a lout from the Gestapo; he pressured the Danish Government into moving Scavenius from Foreign Minister up to Prime Minister; and he replaced Gen. Lüdke, the Army Commander in Denmark, with Gen. von Hanneken, a Nazi and member of the SS. It was one of his typical tantrums, and needless to say it did nothing to make matters any easier.

But time was running out for the Germans. Three things happened in the fall of 1942 that ended their winning streak and put them on the defensive, the first of which was the British victory at El Alamein, in North Africa. There, from October 23 to November 4, Montgomery's forces fought Rommel's Afrika Korps and beat them back to the west. Then, on the night of November 7–8, British and American forces landed in Morocco and Algeria, and started the squeeze that would finally drive Rommel out of Africa. And finally, on November 19 and 20, the Russians at Stalingrad bottled up and eventually destroyed an entire German army, consisting of twenty-two divisions. These three things were signs of what was to come, and they gave us hope at the time we needed it most. As Sigvald had said, things were going to get a lot worse before they got better, but at least they were moving in the right direction.

Chapter Eight

That was a cold winter, so cold that the Sound between Denmark and Sweden froze over. From Copenhagen to the nearest point in Sweden is about eighteen miles, but from Elsinore, in the north, the distance is only two and a half miles. Several people tried to escape from the country by walking over the ice; between twenty and thirty made it, and a number of others didn't. Disorientation, snow blindness, and shifting ice floes were the main enemies, and some people either froze to death or disappeared in the mushy water where the ice had thinned. From Elsinore it was a comparatively easy crossing, but from Copenhagen it was something else again.

On Wednesday, January 27, 1943, the war took on a wholly new aspect. I had gone to bed early, for once not having anything to do with Ole and the others, and I was awakened by the concussion of a series of explosions. As I became fully conscious I realized there was a steady drone behind the thudding. In other words, this wasn't the work of saboteurs; it was an air raid. I bounded out of bed and into the living room, where I saw that my mother had pulled aside the blackout curtain and was crouched by the window, looking at the sky. A pale light touched the outlines of her face and was reflected in her eyes.

"It's down by the harbor," she said. "It must be the Naval dockyard."

I joined her, and saw the flickering glow to the east. She still smelled warm from the bed, but she was trembling as though she were cold.

"Is it the British?" I asked.

"How can you tell? I suppose it must be."

"They wouldn't bomb the dockyard. It's more likely Burmeister & Wain." This was a large machine works, which had been turning out Diesel engines for the German submarines. It had been considered a target for sabotage, but was too formidable for our limited equipment.

My father came in, tying the sash on his dressing gown. "What's going on here?" he asked.

"It seems to be an air raid," my mother replied. "Jens thinks they're bombing Burmeister & Wain."

"Who is 'they'?"

"The RAF, of course. Who else?"

"They have their nerve. Don't they know we're not at war?"

My mother bit her lips together, then said, "No, but you may recall the Germans are."

"That's another kettle of fish entirely. We still have our sovereignty, and until our Government declares war on someone we are at peace."

"Dear God in Heaven, how can you say that?" she cried. "Can't you see what's happening?"

"Until we declare war we are still at peace," he repeated.

"And the British have no right to come bombing our factories in the middle of the night." With that he turned, and went back to bed. My mother watched him go, then looked at me. She was quiet for several seconds.

"Are you all right?" she asked, at last.

"Of course," I replied. "What do you mean?"

"What you're doing."

"I don't know what you're talking about."

"Yes you do, but we won't press it. Just don't take any silly risks."

"I guess everything is a risk, isn't it?" I said.

She hesitated, then said, "Yes. I guess it is." She squeezed my arm hard, then stood up and went to join my father.

It was the Burmeister & Wain works that the British bombed, and it was a not-so-subtle hint for our saboteurs to get to work. It would be to our advantage to have people on the ground do the job, because they could place the explosives where there'd be minimum risk of civilian casualties, whereas in a bombing nobody could ever be sure who might or might not be hurt. But one way or another, they were saying, those places that are helping the German war effort are to be wrecked. Better you than us, but someone's going to do it. It was the first—and, as it turned out, the last—time the British bombed an industrial target in Denmark; our people took the hint and, with considerable help from the RAF, British Intelligence, and the BBC, mounted a sabotage campaign of staggering proportions. In January there were fourteen sabotage actions, in February twenty-nine, and in March sixty, and from there the number steadily increased to a final total of four thousand, seven hundred and four. The saboteurs considered themselves an arm of the RAF, and were proud of it.

The mention of Intelligence leads me to something I didn't

know at the time, because for obvious reasons it was a highly guarded secret from everyone except those directly concerned. Much later, it came out that one of Denmark's biggest contributions to the Allied cause was in the field of military, and especially naval, intelligence. German ship movements in the North Sea, the Baltic, and all through the area were reported with great speed and accuracy by members of the so-called inactive Danish armed forces, either by direct wireless or by way of Sweden. Items like that get lost in the telling of the more colorful events, but they are often more important than any of the rest. There is probably a whole book in itself on the British Naval officer who, with Danish cooperation, spent the war on a small island off the coast, identifying and reporting German ships as they went past.

One more item of political note, and then we'll get on with the story: In March the Germans, apparently to maintain the fiction that Denmark was really a free country, allowed general elections to be held, and on the 23rd the people went to the polls and returned a thumping defeat for the Danish Nazis. Of the hundred and forty-eight seats in *Folketinget*, or Parliament, a hundred and forty-three went to adherents of the democratic Government, three to Nazis, and two to members of the peasants' party. The Germans tried to make this out a victory for the collaborationists, but nobody was even slightly fooled. It was a pro-Danish, anti-Nazi vote, with the Nazis coming away with 2.1 per cent of the total ballots cast. There was muted glee during the two minutes of silence on April 9, almost as though a tiny revenge had been wrought.

That spring the British began to supply us with arms and explosives, and the boost in our morale was almost as great as the boost in our firepower. You have a sort of tentative feeling when you're using a homemade gun, even if you've shot it several times and know it works, and one made by a professional feels a lot better in your hand. The same goes for hand grenades: one made out of a plastic soap container and a makeshift fuse doesn't give you half the confidence of a little iron pineapple with a regular pin to pull. The homemade arms served their purposes, certainly, but the real ones were a lot more congenial for the users. Of course, to the people they hit it was a matter of indifference who'd made the weapon, but that's neither here nor there. *We* felt better, which at the time was all that mattered.

Ole and I took part in some of the early recoveries of arms drops, and while we later managed to refine our technique there was never a drop I know of that wasn't a hairy experience. Too many things could, and often did, go wrong, and you never knew until you were home in bed if you'd gotten away with it. And even then, you couldn't be a hundred per cent sure.

The system was that we waited to hear a certain code word on the evening BBC broadcast; that would inform us the drop was on for that night, and we would go to a prearranged place at a prearranged time. The specific place of the drop was indicated by the code word; there were a number of possibilities.

Our first one occurred on June 3, and of all inconvenient times it was the night of my mother's fortieth birthday. What with the rationing and the food shortages and all, it wasn't possible to have much of a party, but she'd asked a couple of neighbors to come and help cheer her on what apparently was a depressing birthday. (She maintained that her thirtieth was the worst, but that this one ran it a close second.) She'd originally asked only the Jørgensens and the Jakobys, but then Mrs. Bjøl got wind of it, and she felt she had to ask the Bjøls, too.

"I will not have that woman in my house," my father said, when she gave him the guest list. "She'll read our mail and go through our bankbook and rifle the dresser drawers. We won't have a secret in the world after she's left." He paused. "Or a crumb of food either, for that matter."

"Oh, don't be silly," my mother said, as she went around lighting the candles. "She's not that bad. Besides, they're bringing their own food, so all you'll have to provide is the beer and snaps."

"All?" he replied. "*All?* That's the whole bloody party."

"Well, after all it *is* my birthday," she said quietly.

"Uh," he said, stunned. "I'm a lout. I forgot." He got up and left the room, and reappeared a moment later with a small package, which he gave to her. "I'm sorry," he said. "Happy birthday." She opened it, and disclosed a thin silver necklace with a small pendant. She embraced him and wept a little, and as she put the necklace on I thought she looked considerably younger than forty.

The radio had been turned on (the news in Dutch came before ours, and we sometimes practiced learning Dutch by listening to it), and now came the boom-boom-boom-BOOM, and we adjusted the dial for minimum jamming and were quiet. First came the news, all of which was good: The Russians were rolling the Germans back on the Eastern Front, and in Africa the Allies had just about finished mopping up the Afrika Korps and were getting ready to invade either Sicily or Italy, or wherever. Since it was they who now had the initiative, they were able to keep the Germans and Italians guessing. There was special news for Danes and a talk by Christmas Møller, and then the announcer said, "And now for our birthday greetings for the day." I leaned forward intently, and my mother seemed to hold her breath with the thought she might be mentioned, but as he read off the names and hers wasn't among them, she relaxed. I, however, became tense, because I'd heard the name Helmut, which was a code word for a drop.

I was still wondering how I was going to make my excuse when the guests arrived, and this complicated matters even further. They all brought small token presents for my mother, and a variety of non-rationed foods; my father went to the refrigerator for the snaps and beer, and there was a brief bit of birthday chatter before the subject got back, as it always did, to the news.

"I think the whole thing will be over by this fall," Mr. Bjøl announced. He was a short, pudgy man, with wispy blond hair that hung like a cloud over his round, shiny head. "The British and Americans will sweep up through Italy and take Berlin, and that'll be that. There'll be no stopping them."

"I'm afraid you're a little optimistic, Hans," Mr. Jørgensen replied. He made an odd conversation partner with Mr. Bjøl because he was lean as a stork, and seemed to arch over him as he talked.

"Do you know anything that'll stop them?" said Mr. Bjøl, looking up at him. "They've got everything stacked in their favor."

"I know what I hope will stop them," put in Mrs. Jakoby. "I hope Hitler should drop dead this minute, and all the rest of his crew." She knocked wood. "I won't sleep nights until they're every one of them dead."

"So go shoot them," said her husband. "Anything to let you get a little sleep."

"Very funny," she replied. She had a thin face, and her dark eyes looked as big as lumps of coal. "Mark my words, the day will come when you'll wish I had." She knocked wood again.

"So go do it," said Mr. Jakoby, with a laugh. "Who's stopping you?"

I decided the time had come to get away. I went to my mother and, in a low voice, said, "I'm sorry, Mother, but I have to go."

She looked startled, and touched the pendant on her necklace. "I'm sorry, too," she said.

"Something's come up—at the University—I'd forgotten about an exam. . . ." I wasn't doing very well, but I felt I owed her some sort of explanation.

"Yes, I know," she said. "Run along. And be careful."

"I will." Turning to the others, I said, "I hope you'll all excuse me."

"What's this?" said my father, appearing with his arms full of bottles. "Where are you going?"

"I'm sorry," I said. "I just remembered—"

"He has a special exam," my mother put in, still touching her pendant. "It's something the University just sprung on him."

"You didn't mention it earlier."

"I know. I forgot. I'm sorry." I moved toward the door, and took my cap from the rack.

"If you ask me, you sound like one of those Freedom Fighters," Mr. Bjøl observed. "They're always running around—"

"Hans, don't be absurd!" my mother said sharply. "Jens wouldn't do anything like that, and you know it!"

"Nobody knows anything," said Mr. Bjøl. "Everything in the world is pure conjecture."

"Well, I can tell you *one* thing I know," Mrs. Bjøl put in. "I know Gerda Rasmussen's daughter has been going out with a German soldier, and there are those who think she may have to marry him. And he isn't even an officer!" Mrs. Bjøl was plump, like her husband, and she had a Buddha-like habit of folding her hands beneath her paunch, which in her case was something of a reach. Even rationing hadn't thinned her down, which nobody could understand. Most people were thin as pencils.

"Conjecture," her husband replied. "Until you've seen the marriage license, it's pure conjecture."

I went out, and the last thing I saw was my mother, still touching the pendant at her neck.

I met Ole on a small side street branching off Strøget, and in a few minutes I recognized the car coming toward us. We got in, and saw Sigvald and the same driver up front, but the moment we started off I realized this wasn't the same car as we'd had before; this one was really running on wood—or peat, or lignite, or some other substitute. The engine seemed to flutter, like a wounded bird.

"What happened to the other car?" I asked.

"One of those things," Sigvald replied. "It didn't go quite fast enough."

"Were they caught?"

"That's right."

"Who was in it?"

"Nobody you'd know."

It occurred to me I was asking questions that were really none of my business, so I stopped. It also occurred to me that if the other car hadn't been fast enough this one could only be worse, and all I could do was hope we wouldn't get in a spot where speed was important. I came to realize, later, that you never go into any operation as well equipped as you'd like; there's always something makeshift or second-rate or missing, or, if it was supposedly perfect when you started, it invariably breaks down.

Our drop site was to the northwest of Copenhagen, near the lake between Birkerød and Holte. I wondered why they chose a place so close to the shore, since it required that much more pilot accuracy to keep the drop from being lost in the water; then I realized it cut down on the number of sides on which we were vulnerable, and gave us at least a hope of escape if we were cornered. What made these drops so hairy was their timing; the German radar or direction finders would spot the plane the minute it entered the area, and then, while it circled waiting for us to flash the guiding lights, the Germans would be homing in from all sides. Twenty minutes was the most you could allow for the whole business, and if you could do it in an almost impossible ten, so much the better.

The area to the north of Copenhagen is good farmland, interspersed with lakes and forests, and while it could never be called hilly, it undulates a bit more than the rest of the country. Most of Denmark, especially Jutland, is as flat as a flounder. Our area was just beyond the city limits, but when we turned off the lights and drove slowly to the edge of the lake we could as easily have been at Loch Ness. There was no growl of traffic and no loom of city lights; the only sounds were of a night bird calling in a tree by the shore, and the chirp of a cricket in the grass. The driver put his head out the window and listened.

"He's not here yet," he said.

"Just as well," said Sigvald. "Neither is Gloria."

"*Gloria?*" I put in. "Who's she?"

"It's someone's cover name," Sigvald replied. "He's supposed to be here to help us. Keep an eye out back, and see if anything's coming."

Ole and I craned our necks to look through the rear window, but all we could see were the dim outlines of trees and bushes—plus, of course, our quietly smoking woodburner. I renewed my hope we'd have no cause to use speed.

"Damn," said the driver, suddenly. "There's the plane."

We listened, and could hear the faraway drone of an airplane. It came closer, then turned and receded; came closer again, and went off, like a mosquito in the middle of the night. It was a large plane, possibly a Lancaster or a Halifax. Sigvald got out of the car.

"When he comes back, we've got to signal him," he said. "We can't wait around."

"There aren't enough of us," said the driver. "How do you make a cross with four lights?"

"Make a box instead," Sigvald replied. "Let him aim for the center."

"How does he know that? He'll be looking for a cross."

"He'll have to guess," replied Sigvald, irritably. "I can't come up with all the answers."

"If we wait for Gloria, then we'll have enough," said the driver. "There's no point trying to do with only four people, and two of them—" He didn't finish the sentence, but we knew what he was thinking. Two of them greenhorns.

"If we wait for Gloria we may all wind up dead," Sigvald replied. "Come on, let's light up for him."

We got out of the car and the driver passed out flashlights, and then Sigvald stationed us at four corners of the area, with instructions to shine our lights upward when he told us to. We waited while the noise of the airplane got louder, and then saw the beam of Sigvald's light stabbing the darkness. He was giving the code letter for the drop, and after what seemed like a long time we saw the answering blink in the sky. It was like a traveling star that stammered as it went. "All right," Sigvald called. "All of you light up." We shone our beams upward, and the engine noise became louder and louder; then it cut to almost nothing as the pilot put the plane in a glide, and we could actually hear the whistling of the wind in its wires. Then the engines roared again, so loudly I thought my head would burst, and the plane zoomed up and into the night sky. I saw the blue flame of its exhausts, and its silhouette like that of a monstrous bird against the stars. In the beams of our lights we saw a dim, ghostlike thing hanging above us; for a moment I had a picture of a witch, her cape flying, riding a thick, black broomstick. Then it came down, fast, and the canister hit the ground with a thud, while the gray-green parachute settled slowly around it and enveloped it as an octopus does a crab. There came the sounds of others, landing farther off. We rushed toward the nearest one, and while I was clawing at the folds of the parachute Sigvald gave Ole a shovel and told him to start digging.

"Digging?" said Ole. "For what?"

"To bury it, of course," Sigvald replied. "Stop talking, and dig."

The canister was a tube, between five and six feet long, and to open it you undid a catch-lock and pulled two handles, with which the sides fell apart. The interior was painted a dark reddish brown, and neatly stowed in it were packages marked "PE#2," which stood for plastic explosives; boxes of fuses and detonators, with instructions for their use; one bazooka, with six projectiles; four rifles, two Sten guns, and, in padded zipper bags, various items of radio transmission and receiving apparatus. There were also pistols and hand grenades, as well as boxes and belts of ammunition, and assorted pamphlets and instructions. One of these, I saw, was entitled "How to Derail a Locomotive," and I resolved to read it the first chance I had.

"Just like Christmas, isn't it?" Sigvald said, grinning, as he picked up the bazooka. "Come on, let's get these stowed."

Ole dug like a frantic woodchuck, while Sigvald and the driver and I hurried back and forth between the canister and the car, taking as much as we could carry each time. For those who have never tried it, I can testify that it is not easy to run when your arms are full of rifles, pistols, grenades, and ammunition, because the load joggles and slips and clatters loose, and you're constantly dropping things if you try either to carry too much or to go to fast. It's a neat balance that has to be struck, and it took me a while to find it. Finally, when we'd stowed everything in the car and were going back to help Ole bury the empty canister and parachute, the driver put up his hand.

"Listen!" he said. "A car!"

We listened, and from somewhere could hear the sound of an automobile.

"It's Gloria," said Sigvald. "Now that we've got the job all done."

"I don't think so," said the driver. "It sounds like a Mercedes."

"They wouldn't send a Mercedes on a job like this," Sigvald replied. "They'd send a squad car, or a fleet of Volkswagens. Let's bury this stuff, and get out of here." I couldn't understand why Sigvald was so sure of himself when the driver was so apprehensive, but Sigvald had never been wrong before, and I felt he must know something the rest of us didn't. And here I learned one of the primary lessons of the whole business, which is never to assume something without being absolutely positive you're right. As it turned out, this time Sigvald was wrong.

We were stuffing the parachute in the hole when suddenly the engine noise became louder; there was a squeal of brakes and four doors slammed, and then someone shouted "*Halt!*" and the whole area was lit up by a spotlight. Sigvald flung himself on the ground behind the canister, pulled a pistol from his belt, and snapped off three shots in the direction of the light, then got up and ran for our car. Ole and I, having learned to carry pistols any time we went out, hit the ground and tried to get in a spot where we could fire, but the light seemed to sear into everything, and I didn't dare raise my head for long enough to aim. I heard the driver shooting nearby, and then there came the ripping snort of a machine pistol, and the driver grunted and was quiet.

There came shots from the right, where Sigvald had run, and then there was a pop and tinkle of glass, and the searchlight went out. I lay still, blessing the darkness, then raised my head and looked around. I saw a stab of flame from Sigvald's gun, and an answering flutter of flame from the German car, and in the silence that followed I could hear the Germans making their way through the grass. I couldn't tell who was who or who was where, and I hesitated to shoot without knowing the target. (Also, to be honest, I knew that to shoot would give away my position, and I wasn't going to do that unless I could be sure to make the shot count.) All sorts of thoughts ran through my mind: I wondered if I could make a dash for it and hide in the water; I wondered if it would do any good to run for the car and try to load the bazooka; and I wondered what my chances would be if I simply headed off into the night. The last was tempting in that I probably would have made it; I myself could escape, at the expense of leaving the others to face the Germans. Well, so much for that, I thought, and found myself strangely calm in thinking it. It occurred to me that I, who had been nervous about pasting labels on soldiers' backs and putting sugar in their gas, was no longer nervous in a situation that could very easily result in my death; I was terrified, but the terror had a strangely calming effect, like an anesthetic that lets you see what's going on without feeling any of the pain. The physical thing the terror did was make my mouth as dry as old leather, so that my lips stuck to my gums. I don't imagine all these thoughts took more than a second or so, but it seemed I had lain there for an hour or two when all at once, from behind the German car, came the clatter of automatic weapons, and flashes of light, and shouts, and one long scream. Then the confusion was total; shadowy figures ran in all directions and stabs of gunfire flickered in the darkness, and I got up and sprinted for our car. I reached it and found Sigvald there, looking across the hood with his pistol raised.

"What's happening?" I asked.

"Gloria finally got here," he replied. "He caught 'em from behind."

Then, as suddenly as it had begun, the shooting stopped, and all I could hear was the pounding of my heart in my ears. Sigvald listened for a few moments, then called, "Gloria?"

"Sigvald?" came back the reply.

"Did you get 'em all?" Sigvald asked.

"I don't think so. Two lit out for the woods."

Cautiously, Sigvald and I came out from behind the hood, and joined other figures coming from the third car. I wondered where Ole was, and had a flash of panic when I realized I hadn't seen or heard him since the shooting started. I called, and was relieved to hear his voice.

"I need some help over here," he said. "I think the driver's had it."

I went to him and shone my light on the driver's face, and while I wasn't an expert on such things I must say he looked dead. Then Sigvald was behind me.

"Let's hurry and get him out of here," he said. "There'll be more Germans any minute."

We dragged the driver to our car, and there was a leaden, floppy feeling to him that told me for sure he was dead. We bundled him in back, where he sprawled among the weapons, then Sigvald got behind the wheel and Ole and I joined him up front. He leaned out his window and said, "OK," and the German car turned on its lights and began to move off. We swung in behind it, and the third car followed us.

"Who's driving the Mercedes?" I asked.

"Gloria," Sigvald replied. "He speaks the best German."

I wondered what this meant, and I wasn't long in finding out. Ahead of us appeared two sets of headlights, coming in our direction, and Sigvald took his pistol from his belt and laid it on the seat between his legs. "Get ready," he said, quietly.

Ole and I brought out our pistols and held them pointing toward the floor, and then we all watched as the headlights came closer, until they were almost abreast of the Mercedes. Then the Mercedes' brake lights glowed red, and we knew he'd been ordered to stop. We held our breaths, trying to hear what was going on ahead, but only the mumble of voices came back to us. Half under his breath Sigvald was muttering, "Come on, come on, come on," and it came to me this was the first time I'd ever seen him nervous.

"Well, his German must be pretty good," Ole observed. "If it weren't, they'd have started shooting by now."

"It isn't the language that's worrying me, it's the uniform," Sigvald replied. "He picked up one of the caps from the ground, but he hasn't got a tunic."

Then the Mercedes began to move, and the headlights shone in our faces, and as we started up Sigvald looked at the oncoming cars, gestured behind us, said *"Immer gerade aus!"* and speeded up to catch the Mercedes.

"What did you say?" Ole asked.

"I just told him to keep going straight," Sigvald replied. "It'll give him something to think about for a while." He glanced in the rearview mirror and saw our other car behind us. "But they won't be fooled forever," he said. "And we'd better start looking for some side streets."

As we came into the northern part of the city Sigvald gave the two–one beep on his horn, and the three cars split up and went in different directions. We turned down a street to the right, and followed a first-right-second-left course until I was completely lost. Then all at once I smelled the water, and realized we were headed back north, along the road that leads to Elsinore. We followed the shore for a while, past small harbors and basins where the fishing boats bumped quietly at their moorings, and then at Rungsted we turned and headed inland. We left the paved road, and after a while I saw a cluster of farm buildings loom up in the darkness. In Danish farms the houses and barns are all lumped together in the form of a U, and when we drove into the enclosure we were almost totally hidden from outside eyes. Sigvald stopped the car and whistled once, and in a moment a man came out of the house and joined us.

If there had been any doubt about the driver before, there was none now; his joints had begun to stiffen, and we had a terrible time getting him out of the car. Ole and the farmer carried him into one of the outbuildings, while Sigvald and I began to load the arms and ammunition into a hayloft. Then the other two joined us, and pretty soon the work was done. I don't think three words had been spoken since we arrived.

We were quiet on the drive back into the city, and I guessed that Sigvald was going over the evening's events and blaming himself for what had happened. There was nothing to be done about it; all you can do in the circumstances is resolve not to make the same mistake again. But he still had the man's family to talk to, and that couldn't have been a cheering prospect. He let us off near Strøget, and drove into the night without a word.

One candle was burning in the living room when I got home, and as I went to blow it out my mother called me softly. I tiptoed to the bedroom door, which was partly open, and when I reached it she said, "I'm glad you're home."

"So am I," I replied.

"Good night," she whispered.

"Good night." I started away, then came back. "I almost forgot," I said. "Happy birthday."

Chapter Nine

Nineteen forty-three had started with the bombing of the Burmeister & Wain shops, and as the year went on the violence grew. The sabotage increased, there were strikes and street fights, and as the food supplies dwindled the people's mood became progressively uglier. The Model Protectorate was very clearly getting the thin end of the stick, with our protectors stripping us of everything they needed and demanding more every day. Coffee, tea, tobacco, and butter were rationed and/or nonexistent; soap was almost unobtainable, and fuel reserves were down to almost nothing —except of course for German use. Also, since they were doing poorly on the war fronts (Italy was knocked out of the war in July) they were increasingly nervous, and overreacted in a way that made matters worse than before. In order to deal with the strikes and street fights, they brought back five or six hundred Danish Nazis from the Russian front and organized them into the so-called Schalburg Corps, a sort of counter-sabotage unit. They literally ran riot through the streets, murdering, raping, looting, and bombing, and if Werner Best thought they would keep the population quiet, he soon found out the opposite. The Danish people's loathing for these goons was so intense that the violence increased, and what had been small strikes spread into larger ones. During one demonstration a German officer opened fire on the crowd, and they turned on him in a howling rage and beat him to death.

One example should suffice to show how both the Danes and the Germans felt about the Schalburg Corps. One evening, at the end of the work day, a German soldier tried to get aboard a crowded tram. Nobody would move to make room for him; they just stared at him with stony faces and held their ground, and as the tram was about to move he flung out his hands and said, in broken Danish, "Please! I not traitor—I not Schalburg man!" There was a pause, then the people moved to make room for him, and he got aboard.

I am slowly getting around to Ingrid Nielsen, my sometime girlfriend, but I want to do a little explaining along the way. Since 1912, Denmark has celebrated American Independence Day, the Fourth of July. The custom started after many Danes emigrated to America, and their friends and relatives wanted to have something to share with them. They felt that by celebrating the Fourth they would be doing what the others were doing at the same time, and there grew up a feeling of warmth about the whole occasion. Needless to say there was no overt celebration this year, but there did seem to be a burgeoning of patriotic skullcaps, both of the red-and-white Danish variety and of the red-white-and-blue type of the RAF and Allied colors. Then suddenly, on July 9, came the German edict: No more patriotic skullcaps. *Punkt.*

Period. *Verboten*. With everything else that was going on, people tended to treat the edict lightly, but as it turned out the Germans were serious.

I was crossing Town Hall Square about two days after the ban went into effect, and as I came to where Strøget joins the Square I saw that a crowd had gathered. I veered toward it, and the first thing I saw were the white caps of two Danish policemen, and one of them had a German officer at his elbow. The other was looking at the crowd and telling them to move on, but he was saying it in the perfunctory way of a policeman who feels he has to say something, so I moved closer. People were craning their necks to see, and one youth was leering at the German officer's back with an expression of such hatred that it's a wonder the man didn't feel it. I could see now that the German—an SS man, as it turned out—was supervising the arrest of someone, and when I got still closer I saw who it was. It was Ingrid, standing with her back to a tub of ivy beside a building; she was wearing a sort of tweed suit, and her eyes were wide but her mouth was defiant, and I could just barely see, through the swept-back curls of her hair, the rim of her RAF beret. The policeman had his notebook out, and was presumably writing down her name and address, while the SS man stood by and watched. Then slowly, as though searching the crowd for more skullcaps, the SS man turned around, and I was horrified to find myself looking into the cold eyes of Standartenführer Schlemmer, whom I'd last seen while pointing a gun at him outside the movie theater. It was too late to duck; all I could do was return his stare and hope my face had been well enough covered that night. He continued to look at me, apparently searching his memory, then his eyes moved on, and I was able to look back at Ingrid. I saw the Danish policeman fold his notebook and gesture for her to remove the beret, and she swept it off her head and into her pocket, and walked away. I forced my way through the crowd until I reached her side.

"Hello," I said.

She looked at me, and I could see a glisten of perspiration on her upper lip. "Well, hello!" she said. "Where'd you come from?" She kept on walking, and I went alongside.

"I was just crossing the Square," I said. "Can I get you something?"

She glanced at me again. "Like what?"

"I should think you'd need a drink."

She hesitated. "You're sure you're not busy."

"Of course I'm not busy! I want to talk to you."

"It's been a long time, hasn't it?"

"That's what I want to talk about." All the feeling I'd once had for her, and thought I'd lost, now came flooding back. "I really—I mean, I do." Here I go again, I thought. The minute I try to make a point with a girl, I get tongue-tied. "Please," I concluded, lamely.

She raised her eyebrows in a gesture that wasn't quite a shrug. "All right," she said. "Since you put it that way."

We went to a cafe, and I ordered two beers. "Would you like a snaps to go with it?" I asked.

"No, thanks. This should do the trick."

I cleared my throat. "I hardly know where to begin," I said.

For the first time she smiled. "I know what you mean."

"I mean—well—I hope you know how badly I feel about standing you up."

"So you wrote."

"There was honestly nothing I could do about it. Not a single thing in the world."

"I understand that."

"Then why didn't you answer me?"

"I didn't understand it then. I do now."

"Oh. Well—I guess it was a misunderstanding, then."

She smiled again. "I guess it was."

"I mean, you told Ole I was an odd duck, or something like that, and I thought—"

"Did Ole tell you that?"

"I guess he must have. How else would I know?"

She sipped her beer, and looked into the glass. "That was a shabby thing to do," she said at last.

"Didn't you say it?"

"I may have, but I didn't mean it to sound that way."

"How did you mean it to sound?"

"I don't know. I don't exactly remember."

This left us pretty much where we'd started. "I guess it's one thing or the other," I said. "Either you think I'm an odd duck, or you don't." And *that* sounded wrong the minute I'd said it, but there was no way to take it back.

"Maybe it's a little bit of each," she said. "I don't know."

I took a deep breath, and looked for another topic of conversation. "How's your father?" I asked.

She looked at me. "All right. Why?"

"I just wondered. How's he going to react to your little—ah—brush with the law?"

"With any luck, he won't know about it."

"What are they going to do to you?"

"The policeman kind of hinted nothing would come of it. He sounded awfully ominous, but under his breath he told me it was just a warning."

"That's good."

"I don't think my father would do anything, anyway."

"Why not?"

"Did you know he was posted by the Resistance?"

I feigned amazement. "What do you *mean*?"

"They listed him as a reserved-seat holder for Nazi films."

"And was he?"

"He claims it was all a mistake." She looked into her glass again. "Ever since the Allies started winning, he's been hedging his bets. I hate to say it, but I think he's an opportunist. He calls it being a realist, but that's the nicest thing you could say."

"Well, at least he's not a Nazi."

She was quiet for a moment, then said, "No, at least he isn't that."

I saw an opening, and leaped at it. "Do you think he'd let me in the house?"

She looked up from her glass. "For what?"

"For to pick you up. For a date."

Her face softened, and something turned over inside me. "I thought you'd never say it," she said.

"Tonight?"

"Tonight. What time?"

"Uh—" Suddenly, I realized I had to listen to the BBC, and if any signal came over I'd have to cancel the date. "Damn," I said. "I don't know."

"After the BBC, perhaps?"

I looked at her, and although we both knew what she meant, neither of us acknowledged it. "That's not a bad idea," I said. "I hate to miss the evening news."

"So do I."

I continued to look at her, and then, feeling like the super international spy of all time, I said, "After the BBC it is, then."

We went to Tivoli, and danced at the same place we had before. As we were walking home, she took my arm and held it close, and said, "I was glad to see you today."

"I was glad to see *you*," I said.

"I thought I might never see you again."

"Me, too."

"That's silly, isn't it?"

"It certainly is."

"Do you know why I told Ole you're an odd duck?"

I'd been hoping we'd stay off that subject. "No," I said. "I can't imagine."

"Because you never once even made the slightest pass at me. Most boys I go out with, they've got their engines racing before we even leave the house."

I cleared my throat. "Well—" I began.

"I'm not objecting, mind you," she went on. "I think it's a wonderfully refreshing change. But at first it made me wonder if there was something wrong with me, or—well—"

"Something wrong with me," I supplied.

"Not *wrong*, just different. Now, with Ole, for instance —" She paused, and gave a small laugh. "With Ole, it's sort of like a track meet."

I didn't want to hear anything about her and Ole, or for that matter about her and any other boys. At the same time I had a strange urge for self-punishment, and couldn't stand *not* knowing. "I gather Ole's quite a lover," I said.

She laughed again. "I wouldn't go so far as to say that. Energetic, certainly, but . . ." She left the sentence unfinished, and for some reason I felt better. It occurred to me I might gain more in the long run by staying not exactly aloof, but restrained, and different.

"I just don't believe in that sort of thing," I said, wishing briefly I knew how Ole did it. "I think conquests like that are Pyrrhic victories." If asked to analyze that statement I'd have had trouble, but it sounded good at the moment.

"You're absolutely right," she said. "But I didn't mean to imply Ole's made any conquest. He just tries awfully hard."

"I'm sure he does," I replied, feeling immeasurably better. "He's that type." I fought down an urge to break into a dance step.

We were on the bridge that crosses the lake toward her house, and all at once she stopped, turned to me, and said, "All right—if this is the way it has to be." With that she put her arms around my neck, pressed herself close, and gave me a kiss that almost literally welded us together. I reciprocated, holding her so tightly I almost lost my balance, and for what may have been several minutes we teetered there, making only very small noises. All sorts of things ran through my mind, and I tried to think of some better place we could be, but nothing practical occurred to me so I continued as I was, not wanting to let her go. Standing upright on a bridge in the middle of the city might not have been ideal, but it was a lot better than nothing, and Ingrid was a lot better than even my wildest dreams had made her out. It's funny what your mind does at times like that; part of it is analyzing, part of it is simply enjoying, and part of it is probing ahead, wondering what the next step may be. The first two were easy; it was the next step that I couldn't figure out. Finally we relaxed, and stood with our noses touching, looking into each other's eyes and breathing deeply.

"My," she said at last.

I swallowed. "I couldn't have put it better myself."

She laughed. "Some odd duck."

"Any complaints?"

"On the contrary."

"You know something? You taste like honey, and I mean that literally."

"So do you."

Silence.

"Where do we go from here?"

"Where do you want to go?"

"Uh—" The tattered remnants of my restraint crept back, and I said, "Where is there *to* go?"

"I guess that's up to you."

"I mean . . ."

Silence.

"You mean?" she prompted.

"I mean—I mean, did you mean long-range, or immediate?"

"For immediate, I have to go home. For long-range, that's up to you."

"In *that* case . . ."

"In that case?"

"In that case, I'd like to see more of you."

"I think that could be arranged."

"Good."

Silence.

"You *are* an odd duck, but I love you."

"Then it's worth it."

"It's worth it what?"

"What do you mean, it's worth it what? You said you love me, so I said it's worth it being an odd duck."

Her mouth tightened slightly. "Do I have to drag *everything* out of you?"

"I don't know what you're talking about."

"All right. Forget it." Her tone went flat.

I could sense something was slipping away from me, and I began to panic. "Wait a minute," I said, as she started to walk. "What did I say?"

"Nothing," she replied. "That's just the point."

"I must have said something."

"Nope. Not a thing."

I went along beside her, almost pleading. "If only you'd *tell* me—"

"I can't tell you anything you don't feel."

"But *what*? What is it I don't feel?"

"Lord, you must be dense."

"I'm not going to get any less dense with all this double-talk. Tell me what I said that offended you."

"I told you, nothing. You didn't say a thing."

"Then what are you sore about?"

She started to walk faster, and I almost had to trot to keep up with her. "How good is your memory?" she asked.

"Fine, I guess. Why?"

"Then remember back to everything that was said in the last five minutes, and see if there was something you didn't say."

"I didn't get a *chance* to say anything! I was mostly kissing you!"

"Mostly indeed. Think harder."

"About *what*?"

This kind of pointless exchange went on until we reached her house, and I was in a state bordering on nervous collapse. When we got to her door she turned around, put her hands on my shoulders, and said, "Don't give up. I'm sure, if you think hard enough, it's bound to come to you."

"If you'd only give me a *hint*—" I said.

"I've given you all the hint you need. Thank you for a lovely evening. Good night."

The door closed behind her and I reeled off down the street, seriously contemplating suicide. I went back to the spot on the bridge where we'd stopped, and I thought of the poetic justice if I were to jump into the Sø from that very place, then I realized my body would probably be washed up somewhere else, and the point would be lost. Maybe if I left my wallet here, as a marker . . . I stood exactly where I'd stood before, and I went through everything we'd said and done, and I found I could spot the moment her voice had changed. She'd said I was a queer duck but she loved me, and I said then it was worth it, and she'd said—Wait a minute. She hadn't said it was worth *what*, she'd said it was worth *it* what, which meant I should have said something more, because her next remark was did she have to drag everything out of me. I should have said— Oh. Oh, dear, sweet, merciful God! I started to run, and I ran all the way to her house, and I stood in the street and called to her. I didn't know where her window was, or if she even slept on this side, but I knew I had to make her hear.

"Hey!" I called. "Ingrid!" There was no answer, and I said, "Ingrid! I love you, too! Can you hear me? Ingrid, I love you, too!" I said this several times, and then I heard the sound of a window being opened. A face appeared, but instead of being Ingrid's it was her father's.

"Why don't you take an ad in the paper?" he snarled. "Put it on the BBC—hire a skywriter—just let honest people get their sleep!"

"I'm sorry, sir," I said. "Would you call Ingrid for me?"

"No! Get out of here!" He slammed the window shut, and as I walked down the street I reflected that he might have changed his mind about the war, but he still had a long way to go before he'd be lovable in my book. Then I thought of him as a father-in-law, and had a moment of icy despair.

August brought with it a series of events that not only had a drastic effect on the country, but also started my father on the way toward changing *his* mind about the war. As I said earlier, the strikes and sabotage had been growing, and the introduction of the Schalburg Corps, in mid-August, did nothing except heighten the tension. The strikes themselves were less important than their overall harassing effect, and the fact that they goaded the Germans into taking reprisals.

On August 25 and 26 the Jutland railway system was extensively damaged by saboteurs, and for the Germans this was just about the last straw. I should explain that Jutland is the only part of Denmark that is actually connected to the continent of Europe; the rest of the country consists of some five hundred islands of varying sizes, about a hundred of which are inhabited. Jutland, a peninsula that stretches from Germany up toward Norway, was extremely important to the Germans for the transport of troops and supplies to and from their Norwegian occupation forces, and damage to the Jutland railroad system was a direct blow to their war effort. (As a matter of fact, during the so-called Battle of the Bulge sixteen months later, a German division that was being shifted from Norway as reinforcement was delayed ten days by Danish sabotage, and never reached the battle area.)

At any rate, on Saturday, August 28, the Germans handed an ultimatum to the Danish Government, demanding a curfew, martial law, death for saboteurs, a ban on strikes or any public meetings, complete censorship of news under German supervision—in other words, military dictatorship. They gave the Government until four PM that day to agree. Well, even Scavenius couldn't give in to a set of demands like that, so the ultimatum was rejected and the Government resigned. This left Werner Best and General von Hanneken in charge of the country, and von Hanneken moved in to take over the Danish armed forces.

German troops and tanks had been pouring into Copenhagen since that afternoon, and at four AM Sunday they struck. A raging thunderstorm was going on at the time, and when they attacked the Naval dockyard it was hard for a while to tell which noises were made by men and which were made by nature. As with the Burmeister & Wain bombing, my mother and father and I watched from our windows, and saw only the flickering and the glow in the sky; but the noises were different from the bombing, and the rattle of gunfire could be plainly heard. It was an eerie sensation, with the white flashes of lightning counterpointing the red glow of burning oil, and the low roll of thunder punctuated by rifle and machine-gun fire, and I had the momentary feeling we were watching some demented carnival in hell. My father's face was expressionless as he stared out the window.

"It's all so unnecessary," he said, half to himself. "The whole thing is completely unnecessary."

"You mean the rain?" my mother replied, with a faint trace of sarcasm.

He shrugged. "Everything. The shooting. The burning. The killing."

"Have you any better suggestions?"

He was quiet for a while, then said, "I don't know. I've always heard it takes two to make a quarrel, but—" He shrugged again "—now I'm beginning to wonder."

This, for him, was quite an admission, and my mother and I wondered what was coming next.

"There ought to be a law against it," my father went on. "Somehow, someone ought to make a law that people would obey."

"May I say something, Papa?" I put in.

"Of course," he replied. "What?"

"It's a quote from a book, and I think it applies to what you just said."

"Go ahead."

"There's a book written by an American named Steinbeck, and it's called *The Moon Is Down*. It's about the occupation of Norway, although it doesn't say that in so many words, and at one point he has the mayor of an occupied town talking to the German colonel in charge. The colonel has been insisting that people obey the law, and the mayor says, 'You killed six men when you came in. Under our law you are guilty of murder, all of you. Why do you go into this nonsense of law, Colonel? There is no law between you and us. This is war. Don't you know you will have to kill all of us or we in time will kill all of you? You destroyed the law when you came in, and a new law took its place.' "

"Where'd you read that?" my father asked.

Our printing press at the dental clinic had been making copies of the book, but I didn't think I'd say that. "I saw a copy," I said. "I memorized the passage because it seemed to fit so well."

"I'm surprised they let it be printed."

"Oh, it's illegal. That's why I memorized it—I didn't want to carry the book around."

"Just see you don't quote it to the wrong people."

"I think I'm safe here."

"Yes, but you don't know where else."

"Papa, I think you can trust me to be careful," I said, and behind his back my mother and I looked at each other and smiled.

The fight at the dockyard, as it turned out, was quite a battle. Danish sailors held off the Germans until Rear Admiral Vedel's order, for all ships to escape to Sweden or scuttle themselves at the dock, had been flashed on the wireless and the yardarms of the coastal defense ship *Peder Skram*, and appropriate action taken. The sailors barricaded themselves in buildings and fired on the approaching Germans, who had to fall back and call up heavier reinforcements, and all the while ships were either slipping their moorings and heading out, or their crews were opening the seacocks and planting explosives in the bilges. The whole scene was garishly lighted by one ship that drifted across the harbor in flames, casting the glow on the sky that we saw from our windows. In all, twenty-nine ships were sunk and many more damaged beyond repair; thirteen small ships were captured by the Germans, and thirteen escaped to neutral Sweden. As for the Army, it was taken over with little or no resistance; there was some fighting at Sorgenfri Castle, where the King was in summer residence, but that was soon over and he was made a virtual prisoner. Between three and four thousand officers and men were interned, and the Germans also made hostages of several hundred prominent civilians. It was, in short, a complete take-over, and any pretense of political or territorial integrity was abandoned. On Sunday morning, German soldiers (aided by the Schalburg Corps) went through the city with glue pots and posters, proclaiming martial law in the name of General von Hanneken. Gatherings of more than five people, either in public or in private, were forbidden; a nighttime curfew went into effect; strikes, or inducement thereto, were punishable by death; and the use of the mail, telegraph, and telephone was prohibited until further notice. The most succinct sentence in the entire edict ran: "Arms will be ruthlessly used against acts of violence, assemblage of crowds, etc." Hello, Model Protectorate.

Later that same day, Best called a meeting of newspaper editors in his office, and among other things told them that "in this ridiculous little country, the press has inoculated the people with the idea that Germany is weak. . . . The proclamation issued during the night is our answer. From now on, each editor will be responsible with his head for seeing that the people are no longer poisoned."

But not everything was disaster for the Danes that day. At Korsør, southwest of Copenhagen across the island, the motor torpedo boat *Havørnen* was chased by a German destroyer; the captain took evasive action and lured the German onto a reef and subsequent destruction; and then, when other German ships closed in on him, he beached his boat, got all the crew ashore under fire, and formed them up and marched them the sixty miles to Copenhagen, avoiding German patrols along the way.

For sheer dash and comic glory, however, the undisputed honors went to the Coast Guard ship *Hvidbjørnen,* which was at sea when the "escape or scuttle" message was flashed, and so became the inevitable one that didn't get the word. A German patrol ship stopped her and sent over a boarding party, who struck the Danish colors and hoisted the Nazi emblem, and headed the captive ship for Korsør. The crew of the *Hvidbjørnen* slowly sidled back aft and began to loosen their shoes; the captain looked at his watch and after a few moments said, "All overboard," with which his crew flipped over the rail and into the water. As he was kicking off his own shoes, the captain said to the startled Germans: "Better get ready; she'll be blowing up in a few seconds," and with that he joined his men in the water. The Germans panicked and jumped over the side, guns, boots, and all, and there followed the thump of an explosion in the *Hvidbjørnen's* forward section. From under a tarpaulin in a lifeboat came a young Danish sailor, who struck the Nazi flag and ran up the Danish, and then he too went overboard, and the *Hvidbjørnen* shortly sank, her proper colors proudly flying.

Many people were relieved that the masquerade of German benevolence was finally over, but for the Jews it was the beginning of a nightmare. That Sunday evening, when martial law had been declared, Mr. and Mrs. Jakoby came to our house after supper, and Mrs. Jakoby was white with terror. Her hands were shaking so she could hardly hold her glass, and her eyes seemed larger and darker than usual against the pallor of her face.

"Where are we going to *go*?" she kept saying. "Where? Where is there a place in the world these beasts won't follow?"

"I keep telling you," her husband said. "You're as safe here as anywhere. Just don't worry so much, and you'll feel better." He was smaller than she, and faintly sparrow-like, but there was a genial sort of calm that emanated from him.

"Don't worry, he says," she replied. "A lot of help that

is. I could have a hangman's noose around my neck, and he'd say don't worry. Maybe the rope will break—maybe the hangman will fall in love with me I should be so lucky—just don't worry, it'll be all right. I should better have a record that tells me not to worry, I can keep playing it when the Gestapo come for me, God forbid." She reached out one trembling hand and touched the wood of the table.

"I agree with Isaac," my father said. "I think you're being unnecessarily alarmed. In spite of everything, these people really aren't beasts. They're human beings, like everyone else."

"Oh?" said Mrs. Jakoby. "In what way?"

"In every way. All right—they've taken over the country, and there's nothing we can do about it. If they hadn't had all the provocation they might not have done it, but that's neither here nor there. But taking over the country as an act of war is one thing, and deliberately persecuting one part of that country—in the first place, what would they have to gain? It would be stupid. It would be wasteful. It would be all the things they pride themselves on not being."

"They're beasts," said Mrs. Jakoby. "Pure and simple beasts."

"Sarah, you know that's not true. They're musicians, they're scientists, they're—"

"Tell that to the Jews in Germany!" she cut in. "Tell it to the Jews in Poland—Czechoslovakia—Holland—France—Belgium—try to tell some of *those* people how beautiful they are, and see what kind of answer you get! Everywhere they go they bring the stink of death, and there's no reason we should be any different! Already I can smell it in the air!"

"But we *are* different," my father said, patiently. "We're all Danes, and if they were to try to persecute one group of us, they'd have to persecute us all."

"So who's to say they won't?"

"I just told you, it would be wasteful. It would be a waste of time, and of money, and of manpower, and at this point they can't afford to waste anything. They're slowly going down the drain, and all we have to do is sit back and watch."

My mother, who had taken no part in the conversation, now spoke up. "I hope you never have to regret that sentence," she said.

"What is there to regret?" my father replied. "It's just a matter of time."

"That's right," said Mrs. Jakoby. "Just the time it takes to pull a trigger."

"That's what I like, is a nice cheerful soul around the home," said Mr. Jakoby. "You should come to our house once—we got a million laughs."

"You'll have plenty of chance to laugh in Dachau," his wife replied. "They tell me it's a regular comedy festival."

Just for a change she didn't touch wood, and I noticed the omission and later wondered if she blamed that for what subsequently happened. I imagine she probably did.

Chapter Ten

What happened next crept up slowly. There were rumors and straws in the wind, but few people believed them because the Germans denied everything so vehemently, and it seemed too monstrous to be true anyway. It is hard, in retrospect, to say how much you knew about a certain thing at the moment it happened; you find out a lot about it later, and fit the various pieces into place, and then hindsight takes over and you say of course I knew it all the time. But from this remove, things are cloudy, and to be absolutely accurate is impossible.

One straw in the wind, if such it could be called, occurred on September 17, when a group of Germans in civilian clothes broke into the Jewish Community Center and stole the records containing members' names and addresses. Werner Best, when asked about this, shrugged it off as *"eine recht kleine Aktion"*—a minor search for saboteurs—

in spite of the fact that he had already suggested, in a telegram to von Ribbentrop that went on to Hitler, that the Danish Jews be rounded up and sent to a concentration camp. (This, of course, was one of the facts that wasn't known at the time. What also wasn't known until much later was that Best confided his intentions to Georg Ferdinand Duckwitz, his consular officer in charge of shipping operations, and that Duckwitz, unable to live with the whole thing, passed the word to the Danes.)

All we knew, living as we did more or less out of the center of things, was that Mrs. Jakoby was getting more nervous by the day. Every rumor was magnified by her into an impending pogrom, and she began loudly to wonder if there weren't some way she and her husband could be smuggled to England, or Sweden, or any handy non-Nazi country. She kept looking at me as she said it, and I looked back at her as though she were asking me to turn her into a butterfly.

And here I should disgress for a moment. One of the main results of the fall of the Government in August was that it left a vacuum, which had to be filled by something other than the Germans. To this end, the Danish Freedom Council was established in September, and, while it was technically illegal, it was the governing force for the remainder of the war. It was composed of seven men, and they directed and coordinated all the underground activities. The underground, which had been scattered, changed into an organized resistance movement, with chains of command, rules and regulations, and all the trappings of a military organization. Mrs. Jakoby, I think, suspected that I was in some way involved, and was hoping I could work a miraculous escape for her and her husband.

The next straw in the wind was on September 18, when a special detail of Adolf Eichmann's SS men arrived in Copenhagen. Their arrival was not publicized but it became known just the same, and the mere mention of Eichmann's name was enough to freeze the blood of any Jew. He was Hitler's hatchet man, responsible in the end for something like six million deaths. Nothing happened immediately, but the tension went one notch higher.

Then on Friday, September 30, two German transports arrived in Copenhagen harbor, and it shortly became apparent that they were empty, waiting to pick up passengers. And that morning, in the Copenhagen Synagogue, Rabbi Marcus Melchior told his congregation what Duckwitz had revealed to a Danish contact the day before: On Saturday, October 1, the day of Rosh Hashana, the Germans planned to raid all Jewish homes and pack the people on the transports, for shipment to the Theresienstadt concentration camp in Czechoslovakia. The word spread like a brush fire. The number of Danish Jews has been estimated at between six and eight thousand people, and of these ninety-five per cent lived in Copenhagen; by the end of that day almost every one of them had been warned. People telephoned their Jewish friends and acquaintances, then went through the telephone book and picked any names that looked Jewish; others roamed the streets, telling any passersby who appeared likely to be interested; and one man, an ambulance driver, took the day off and went around picking up Jews in his ambulance, taking them to places where they could hide. In this case, the only people who didn't get the word were the Germans; they thought their operation was still a secret.

The only trouble was that not everybody believed the warning. Mr. Jakoby was one of these. Mrs. Jakoby arrived at our house that Friday evening, hysterical and all but incoherent.

"Somebody's got to talk to him!" she wailed. "Somebody's got to kick some sense into his head! Rabbi Melchior himself tells us we should go in hiding, and Isaac Jakoby says he's an alarmist! Isaac Jakoby should tell the Rabbi he's an alarmist? What kind of a madman am I living with?"

"Now, wait a minute, Sarah," my father said. "Did you actually hear Rabbi Melchior say this?"

"Myself, I didn't hear it," Mrs. Jakoby replied. "I wasn't at the service. Bella Oppenheim was there and she heard it, and Moses Katlev, and Ebbe and Olga Abrahamsen. This is no fly-by-night rumor. The Rabbi said it. A hundred and fifty people heard him say it."

"And what did he say?"

"He said there would be no service this morning. To prove the point, he was in street clothes—no robes, no nothing. He said he had information the Germans planned to raid our homes tomorrow, Rosh Hashana, and pick everyone up and send them off to concentration camps. He said—"

"When you say 'our homes,' what do you mean?"

"Jewish homes, what else? Would the Rabbi be talking to Jesuits?"

"But there are no Jewish homes as such. We're all Danes."

She looked at him for a moment with real scorn. "Ole Hansen, you're an idiot," she said. "Well intentioned, perhaps, but an idiot."

"Never mind," my father said. "Go on. What else did he say?"

"He said by nightfall tonight we must all be hiding. The Rabbi of the Copenhagen Synagogue said that, and Isaac Jakoby says he's an alarmist. He says he must have got his information distorted."

"And where did his information come from?"

"Who knows? But would he pass a word like that along unless he believed it? Would he have got where he is if he didn't speak the God's own truth?"

"I'll admit it sounds ominous," my father said. "But look

at it this way—mightn't it be possible that someone set out intentionally to create panic? Someone who knew what a rumor like this would do—isn't it possible that a demented mind could wreak almost as much havoc as if it were actually true?"

"Almost as *much*?" Mrs. Jakoby said, her voice rising. "Almost as much as a concentration camp? Almost as much as the gas ovens? Almost as—"

"Oh, come now," my father put in. "Those gas ovens are rumor, nothing more. Nobody in the twentieth century would be so depraved as to do a thing like that, and you know it. Nobody."

My mother and I had been listening without adding anything to the exchange, and now my mother said, "Mightn't it be a good idea to call Isaac, and see what he has to say? If he can stand up against Rabbi Melchior *and* Sarah, maybe he knows something we don't."

"It'll do you no good," Mrs. Jakoby said. "He's as stubborn as a Galilean jackass."

"Nor will it do any harm," said my father, going to the phone. "I believe we shouldn't panic until we've heard from all sides. Panic is the very last resort." He picked up the instrument, listened, then jiggled the button. "Line's dead," he said.

"Oh, my God, they're coming!" Mrs. Jakoby wailed. "They've shut off the phones, and now they're coming!"

"Not necessarily," my father said. His face was blank as he put the instrument down, and turned to me. "Jens, why don't we go talk to Mr. Jakoby?" he said. "Sarah, you stay here with Herta."

We didn't speak as we went down the darkened street to the Jakobys' house, and I could tell that my father was trying to readjust his thinking. He couldn't yet bring himself to admit what was happening, but he was finding fewer and

fewer ways to deny it. He knocked softly on the Jakobys'
door, and waited. He knocked again, and after a few moments there was a shuffle of movement behind the door.

"Who is it?" came a hoarse whisper.

"It's me, Isaac," my father replied. "Jens and I came to
see you."

The door opened a crack, then swung wider. "Come in,"
said Mr. Jakoby, still in a whisper.

"We tried to call, but our phone is out," my father said,
as we went in. "Do you know if yours is working?"

"It has been," Mr. Jakoby replied, turning on the lights.
"Sarah's been on it most of the day."

"See if it's working now." My father tried to sound
casual, but he gave himself away by trying too hard.

Mr. Jakoby lifted the phone, and listened. He held it to
his ear for what seemed like a long time, and then put it
down. "It seems to be out, too," he said.

My father cleared his throat. "Isaac, I needn't tell you
what a state Sarah is in," he said. "I frankly don't know if
her fear is warranted or if it isn't, but I think something
should be done before she has a complete collapse."

"Like what?" said Mr. Jakoby.

"Like—well, perhaps if you and she were to spend the
night with us, until we see if this thing comes off or doesn't.
Even a small thing like that would ease her mind a little, and
to be honest with you I think she's pretty close to the edge."

Mr. Jakoby shook his head. "What good?" he said. "We
spend tonight with you, and then what? We can't live with
you. If they come for us they come for us, and that's all
there is to it."

"Sarah says you don't believe they're coming," my father
said.

Mr. Jakoby shrugged. "She's worried enough, I shouldn't
make it worse. Frankly I think they'd be insane to do it, but

with a schmuck like Hitler who can tell? Maybe they will."

"But you're not worried?"

"Of course I'm worried! I'm so terrified I can't even spit straight! But that isn't going to help anything, so what point discussing it? Worried—I've been throwing up ever since Sarah left here! What do you think makes me so hoarse?"

My father took a deep breath. "And you wouldn't consider spending just one night with us?"

"I wouldn't give the swine the satisfaction. They want me, they know where they can find me."

"What about Sarah?"

Mr. Jakoby paused, a long pause, then said, "For her, it might not be a bad idea. Tell her I say she should spend the night with you, and I'll see her in the morning."

"And you're sure you won't join her? There's plenty of room."

"I tell you, Ole, I don't think you can run. For Sarah it's one thing—it'll do her nerves good to sleep somewhere else for a change. But for me, if I was to run and hide and then this thing *didn't* come off, I'd never be able to look at myself again. I'd be tripping on my beard for not being able to shave in the morning. A lot of people have been running from Hitler all over the world, and look what happens—they're still running. That's no way to live." Apparently the speech embarrassed him, because he started toward the door to let us out. "But thank you all the same for the offer, and thank you for taking care of Sarah. Tell her I'll see her tomorrow. Tell her Happy New Year for me."

We reported his reaction, tempering it somewhat, to Mrs. Jakoby, and she nodded. "Just what I expected," she said. Her hysteria had passed, leaving her in a slightly stunned condition. "Was our phone working?" she asked.

"Uh—no," my father replied. "As a matter of fact, it wasn't."

She nodded again. "That means they're coming," she said.

"Not really," he said, trying to sound convincing. "There could be any number of reasons for the phones to be off."

She looked at him and smiled in a distant sort of way. "There could be," she said, softly. "But there aren't. I know."

There was clearly no arguing with her, so my mother changed the conversation and suggested she go to bed and try to sleep. Mrs. Jakoby looked at her with the same wispy smile. "Sleep?" she said. "Are you serious?"

"It wouldn't hurt to try," my mother said. "I can give you some hot broth, and——"

"Could you sleep on the edge of a cliff?" said Mrs. Jakoby. "Could you sleep falling out of a tree?"

My mother tried to think of something to say, but couldn't.

"I'll just stay by the window, here," Mrs. Jakoby said. "I might doze a little, but sleep—no, thank you."

"Why do you want to stay by the window?"

"When you've all gone to bed, I can lift the curtain and look out. I don't want they should catch me napping."

We were helpless to do anything; her mind was made up, and that was all there was to it. We went to bed, and I lay staring at the ceiling, wondering what was going to happen. There was an unreal quality about the whole thing that made it hard to think about in a rational way; like the first day of the invasion, it was something you couldn't believe, but your senses told you was actually happening. Or was about to happen. Or might never happen. I heard the Town Hall clock strike eleven, and thought, Well, in an hour we'll know. Or maybe two hours. Three at the most. . . .

Something woke me; I don't know what it was. I heard noises in the living room, and got up and went to the door.

Mrs. Jakoby was moving about in the darkness, picking up her belongings, and she glanced at me briefly and then headed for the front hall.

"Where are you going?" I asked, in a whisper.

"They're here," she replied. "They just stopped in front of our house."

"What are you going to do?"

"Shhh!" she said. "Don't wake your parents." And with that she was gone.

I went to the window and pulled aside the blackout curtain, and by leaning out I could see a large lorry stopped in front of the Jakobys' house. After a while two helmeted men emerged from the house holding a smaller third man between them, and they bundled him into the rear of the lorry. They were about to close the doors when a figure came darting along the sidewalk; it was Mrs. Jakoby, calling something I couldn't understand, and when she reached them they took her by the arms and put her in the lorry. They slammed the doors, got in the front, and drove off. Only then did I realize my parents were looking out the other window. For a while none of us spoke. Then my father turned away.

"They did it," he said, half aloud. "They did it, they did it, they did it." He dropped into a chair, and held his clenched fists against his knees. "The miserable sons of bitches did it." I'd never heard him use language like that before, and it made the back of my neck prickle. Nobody spoke for several minutes, and then he said, "I wonder how many people they caught."

"I guess we'll know tomorrow," I said.

Again nobody spoke, and then my father said, "There must be something we can do."

"For the Jakobys?" I said.

"For the others. It's too late for the Jakobys."

"I have a feeling the Jakobys will be all right," my mother said.

"What makes you think that?" my father asked.

"I don't know. I just have a feeling."

"Herta, I'll tell you something. As of now, I am prepared to believe anything unpleasant I hear about the Germans. Nothing will be too low, or too bestial, or too savage for me to believe. I have tried to give them the benefit of the doubt, but from now on I don't believe there *is* any doubt, and they certainly don't deserve any benefit. Jens, what was that speech you told me, about this being war?"

" 'There is no law between you and us,' " I quoted. " 'This is war. Don't you know you will have to kill all of us or we in time will kill all of you? You destroyed the law when you came in, and a new law took its place.' "

"That's the one. 'You destroyed the law when you came in, and a new law took its place.' All right, then. If that's the way they want it, that's the way they'll have it." There was a pause, while he looked at me in the darkness. "I believe you have connections?" he said, at last.

"Who, me, Papa?" I replied. "I don't know what you mean."

"No, of course not. I mean connections who—well, who aren't eager to see the German cause triumph."

"I must know *someone* like that," I said.

"Well, you can tell him, or them, that if he or they want a volunteer, you know where they can find one."

"If I should see anyone, I'll pass the word," I said, hoping my smile didn't show in my voice.

As it turned out, the Jakobys were the exception. All through that day the Germans raided Jewish homes, and in home after home there was nobody there. Out of, say, seven thousand people, exactly two hundred and two were caught in those first raids, and another two hundred and seventy were later picked up attempting to escape. All the rest were in hiding—except the comparative few who panicked and committed suicide. There was a rash of suicides in the first few days of October, when there seemed no hope even for those who were in hiding, but it then became apparent that the Danes were prepared to risk their own lives to save those of their countrymen, and the panic subsided. The reaction of Danes all over the country was just what my father's had been: By this one act the Germans had made violent enemies out of even the most law-abiding citizens, and united all the various factions against them. Christmas Møller, from London, wrote an editorial for *Frit Danmark* in which he said that "if we desert the Jews in this hour of their misery, we desert our native country"; the Lutheran bishops of Denmark sent a letter to the German authorities denouncing the action, and had the letter read from every pulpit that Sunday along with prayers for the Jews; and Kaj Munk, a minister, poet, and playwright who was known as "the greatest dramatist of the north since Ibsen," preached a sermon in which he described the action as "abominable to the Nordic way of thinking," and called on the church and the country to resist the Germans. If they had set out intentionally to solidify their opposition, they couldn't have done it better.

On October 3 Eichmann himself arrived in Copenhagen, as though that would produce better results. He screamed at Best, who had prematurely sent a telegram to Hitler announcing that Denmark was free of Jews, and he ranted and raved and then left town, leaving orders that the hidden Jews were to be found no matter what. Nevertheless the transport *Wartheland* departed with two hundred and two miserable passengers, and the other one left empty.

Frantically, the Germans decided to try bribes. They

lifted some of the restrictions they'd imposed on August 29, and they offered to exchange their hostages for information about where the Jews were hiding. But both General Goertz and Admiral Vedel, the ranking military hostages, declined to accept freedom under such circumstances; as Admiral Vedel put it: "There is no point exchanging one Dane for another Dane." And that went for the others; nobody would buy his own freedom at the price of someone else's, and none but the Nazis and informers would tell what they knew.

The problem, for the Danes, was what to do with the Jews who were hiding in attics, cellars, barns, garages, churches, hospitals, chicken coops, and woodsheds. The matter of feeding them inconspicuously was a tricky one because of rationing, and it was obvious they couldn't stay in hiding forever, so the main thing was to get them out of the country. Through the efforts of Niels Bohr, the Danish physicist, the Swedish Government had agreed to accept any Jews who could get there; but making the crossing in the face of the German patrols was a chancy business. Still, it was the only answer, and there was one advantage in the fact that the underground had already established lanes of contact with Sweden for the shipment of arms, saboteurs, and the like. The underground, along with most of the rest of the population, pitched in to help the Jews.

In Copenhagen there were three main collecting points where Jews were gathered before being shipped out. One was Bispebjerg Hospital, in the northwestern part of the city; another was the Rockefeller Institute; and the third was a bookshop run by an underground operator named Mogens Staffeldt, directly across the street from Gestapo headquarters in Dagmar House. Staffeldt's shop had been *in* Dagmar House until early September, when the Gestapo took over the whole building; he relocated across the street, and continued his clandestine printing and other activities within spitting distance of the super sleuths. It was considered a particularly good joke that his shop be used as a collection center for Jews.

Several books have been written about the whole rescue operation, so I'll limit myself to that part of it in which I personally was involved. I should add, in passing, that I no longer got my instructions from the tree in the park; it was considered unwise to do anything that required daily repetition of a routine, so a number of different ways were worked out to pass instructions. One, of course, was the BBC; another was a prearranged meeting at Tivoli, where people could stroll and talk together without attracting any attention. Tivoli was probably the handiest, and I imagine that at one time or another it might literally have been crawling with underground operators and their contacts. Nobody ever knew the underground people other than those with whom they were directly involved, and even then their names were not their own. It was a long time before I learned Sigvald's real name, and to this day I know the dentist only as Stig. My cover name was Louis—why, I will *never* know.

It was about four days after the raids that I got a message in my mailbox at the University, telling me to be at Tivoli at two that afternoon. What the message actually said was "Pølser 54." Pølser, or hot dogs, was the code name for Tivoli, and 54 meant 14, or two PM. To disguise our numbers, we added 40—for 1940, the year of the invasion—to everything. It was a beautiful Indian summer day; the trees were russet and yellow, and the fallen leaves were crisp underfoot, and it was hard to believe that at that moment several thousand people were cowering in the darkness somewhere, in terror of their lives. As I entered the Tivoli gardens I thought of Ingrid, whom I'd seen only twice since our date, and I reflected how disruptive the war was for any budding romance. I was on the verge of feeling sorry for myself when I thought again about the Jews, and was ashamed.

As I walked slowly toward the bandstand I was aware that someone was coming up behind me, but I didn't turn around. In a moment Stig was alongside, and without appearing to move his mouth he said, "Can you run a boat?"

"I guess so," I replied. "What kind?"

"Fishing boat."

"I can try. What's the matter with the—"

"Don't ask now. Be at Staffeldt's at eight tonight."

"OK." I remembered my father's offer, and said, "Do you need an extra hand anywhere?"

"Who?"

"My father. He wants to join."

"Is he reliable?"

"He's my father! Of course he's reliable!" It occurred to me that a week ago I wouldn't have made that statement, but now I said it without hesitation.

Stig thought a moment, then said, "Tell him to go to Bispebjerg Hospital any time after six, and ask for Dr. Risom."

"That's all?"

"That's all. If they question him, he should say he's come to have his bony turbinates removed."

"OK."

He veered off, and I continued walking. I made a circuit of the gardens, stopped for a beer, and had just put down my money when I saw, not twenty feet away, a man staring at me. It took me a moment to recognize him, because his face had hardened since I'd last seen him, but I finally realized it was my old Scout leader, Holger Andersen. We stared at one another for several seconds, while my mind raced back over the last few minutes, wondering if he'd seen my encounter with Stig or if he'd been deliberately following me, but I concluded there was nothing I could do about it, so I decided to be casual. I raised my beer glass, said, "Ah, there, Holger! *Prosit!*" and took a drink. He turned, and disappeared in the crowd.

All right, I thought. Is this coincidence, or does he know something, and if he knows something, what is it? I didn't really know anything about him; it was possible he'd been in the *Frikorps*, as Ole and I had theorized, but the fact that we hadn't seen him recently was certainly no proof. His face had the look of a man who's been in combat, lean and unsmiling, with a sort of hollow look around the eyes, but again that didn't prove anything. All I knew for sure was what I remembered of his admiration for the Germans, and all I could deduce from that was that I'd better be doubly careful, and if I saw Holger lurking around me again I'd better tell someone about it. The underground had several ways of getting rid of informers, one of which was the "halfway ticket to Sweden," in which the undesirable was taken in a boat, garoted, and his weighted body dumped in the Sound; but these measures weren't used unless there was concrete proof against him, and in some cases even a trial. A quicker way was simple execution with a pistol, but that had the drawbacks that accompany gunfire. As I said, there were a number of ways of doing it, some of them performed by experts. Through friendly police, we had access to all sorts of talent. But the Freedom Council was very strict about its not being done capriciously, and any action had to be fully justified. As of the moment, I had nothing against Holger that would justify anything other than extreme caution.

I finished my beer, looked at my watch, and realized the first thing I had to do was deliver Stig's message to my father.

After that, I decided, it might not be a bad idea to go to the Royal Naval Museum, or the library, or someplace where I could take a crash course in seamanship and boat handling. I'd never run a boat in my life, and I had until eight o'clock that night to learn.

Chapter Eleven

The scene in the back of Mogens Staffeldt's bookshop was confusion beyond belief. Staffeldt was there, and two men I didn't recognize, and for the rest there were about thirty men, women, and children of varying ages, all of them tired, haggard, and frightened. Some had the vacant, staring expression of people resigned to death; others were nervous and irritable; and the children, a few of whom were infants in arms, were as a group like a herd of cattle about to stampede. Some people had brought belongings with them, and some clutched paper bags out of which they fed crumbling food to the children, but for the most part they were just as they'd been when they received the warning to hide. They resembled refugees from a flash flood who'd not yet reached safety, and at whom the water was lapping.

"You're the boatman?" Staffeldt said to me, as I came in.

"In a manner of speaking," I replied. All I'd been able to learn that afternoon was from a guard at the Royal Naval

Museum, who told me a single-screw ship backs to port, and the rule for buoys is Red Right Returning. When I asked him how, for instance, to start the engine, he said that depended on the boat, and he was equally vague about the directional levers and gears. "It'll all come to you," he assured me.

"Well," said Staffeldt, "so long as you can get to Sweden, that's all that matters."

I swallowed, hard. I don't know what I'd thought when Stig asked me if I could run a boat, but I certainly hadn't thought I'd be going to Sweden. From Elsinore, as I've said, it was nothing, but from Copenhagen it was a matter for a practiced navigator. "Does the boat have a good compass?" I asked.

Staffeldt shrugged. "For all I know, it doesn't have any. The Gestapo picked up the skipper last night, and they may have stripped it. You'll just have to make do."

"Great," I said. "That's the kind of trip I like."

He apparently believed me, because he looked at his watch and said, "I don't know what's keeping Sigvald. He should have been here a half hour ago."

"I heard him say he had a delivery this afternoon," one of the other men said. "It may have taken longer than he thought."

"I remember when my first child was born," said his companion. "Fifteen hours, it took. Stop and go, stop and go. I thought I'd go out of my mind."

"Your wife must have liked it, too," said the first.

"Why do we have to wait for Sigvald?" I asked, to change the subject. I had the feeling Staffeldt was becoming irritated by the reminiscence.

"These children have to be sedated," he told me. "We can't take a chance on their making noise along the way."

As though that had been a cue, one of the infants started to wail, then a slightly older child picked it up, and a third joined in. Within three minutes almost every child in the room was crying, two of them stiffening into convulsion hysterics.

"You see what I mean?" Staffeldt shouted, above the din. "We've got to get them quiet!"

"My God, even the Gestapo will hear this," said the man whose wife had had a long delivery. "Can't you make them stop?"

"With what—a bedtime story?" said Staffeldt. "If you have any ideas, I'd be glad to hear them."

The man looked around at the shrieking children and shook his head. "I wouldn't know where to begin," he said.

The back door opened and Sigvald slipped in, carrying his small black bag. He said nothing as he opened the bag, produced a hypodermic needle and small bottle, and then, holding the bottle to the light to make sure he got no air bubbles, filled the hypodermic. He went to the nearest child, indicated to its mother to hold it tightly, then slipped the needle into its arm, moved the plunger a fraction, and withdrew the needle and went to the next. Some of the mothers objected, and these Sigvald passed over until he'd finished with all the others; then he returned to them and, with quiet coaxing, persuaded them to relent. The crying, which had reached a violent crescendo during the injections, now eased off, and some of the children were becoming drowsy. Sigvald looked around the room, then turned to Staffeldt.

"All right," he said. "Better get them started."

"How long will it last?" Staffeldt asked.

"The sedation? I haven't the faintest idea."

"I mean, an hour—two—three—what?"

Sigvald took a deep breath, and lowered his voice. "I had to guess," he said. "Maybe three, but I can't guarantee. I'm just praying I didn't give anyone an overdose."

"Oh," said Staffeldt. "I see."

"Yes. Happy landing." Sigvald snapped his bag shut, gave me a quick nod, and went out into the night.

"All right then, let's get going," Staffeldt said. "Max, you take Louis and as many as you can squeeze into the hearse, and Olaf, you take the rest in the truck. Let's start with Max."

I wasn't used to hearing my cover name, and it was a moment before I realized that I was Louis. Max, the one who'd been reminiscing about his wife, beckoned to me, and we went out back while Staffeldt organized the refugees. A large, black hearse was backed up against the building, and beyond it was a Carlsberg Beer delivery truck.

"How'd you get gas for these?" I asked, as Max opened the back door of the hearse.

"There are ways," he replied. "We have a supply."

"And you're not stopped on the street?"

"We haven't been yet."

We managed to get a dozen people in the back of the hearse, and as we started off Max said, "You should have seen the funeral we had today."

"Oh?" I said. "Who died?"

"Nobody. We had a whole mess of people hiding in a church, and couldn't figure how to get 'em out until someone suggested a funeral. So we dummied up a service and had about fifteen people come, and when it was over a hundred and fifty people left. Biggest damn funeral procession you ever saw."

"Where'd you take them?"

"Elsinore. There's a group there called the Elsinore Sewing Club, and they get people across in jig time."

"Is that where we're going?" I asked, hoping for the shortest possible crossing.

"No. We're going to Rungsted."

"Then where?" There is no Swedish port directly opposite Rungsted.

"You know Hven?"

"I've seen it on a map." It's an island in the Sound, about five miles offshore.

"When you're at Hven, you're in Swedish waters. After that, you can make for Landskrona, or—" He shrugged "— just head for the nearest beach. It depends on how your time is looking. Once you're in Swedish waters, it doesn't really matter."

"It's the first five miles that count," I said.

"That is correct. Five bloody miles. But for an old salt like you, that should be no sweat."

"Who told you I was an old salt?" I asked.

He looked at me. "Aren't you?"

"I've never run a boat in my life."

He looked back at the road, and sighed. "Ah, well," he said. "You're young. You'll learn."

"I hope so."

"Can you steer a compass course?"

"I told you, I've never run a boat in my life. Anyway, Staffeldt said there might not be a compass."

He was quiet for a moment, then put his head out the window and looked at the sky. We were passing along a wooded stretch of road, but a few stars were visible overhead. "You can steer by the stars," he said, settling back. "You know how to find the North Star?"

I felt like a complete idiot. "No."

"Well, I'll show it to you. Keep it to port going over, and to starboard coming back, and you'll have a breeze. You can't miss."

I paused, cleared my throat, and said, "Which is port, and which is starboard?"

"You weren't fooling, were you?" he said gently. "You really don't know anything."

"I've never had any cause to learn. I think port is left, but I'm not sure."

"That is correct. Port is left, and there are four letters in each word. It is also red, the color of port wine. Remember that, and you shouldn't have too much trouble with starboard."

"Thank you," I said.

We drove in silence for a while. I noticed, as we went along the shore, that there didn't seem to be as many boats as before, and when I remarked about it Max said, "Yes. The Germans try to think of everything. Just before the raids, they issued an order that all boats be hauled from the water and taken inland. That was to prevent the Jews escaping by sea. But they exempted fishing boats, so that's what we're using."

"It's almost like a game, isn't it?" I said. "See which side outwits the other."

"Ask the Jews, and they'll tell you if it's a game or not."

"I guess that's right." I listened, to see if I could hear any sounds in the rear, but everything was quiet, and I could only hope it would stay that way until we got into Swedish waters. The last thing I needed was to have the children wake up and start screaming again.

We went through Rungsted, then took a small rutted road that cut through the trees toward the water. Max brought the hearse to a stop in a clearing, set the brake, and took a flashlight from under the seat. "Come on," he said, and got out.

As I got out my side, I saw the Carlsberg Beer truck come to a stop behind us. Max went around to the back of the hearse, opened the door, and in a quiet voice said, "Just a few more minutes. Wait here until we get back."

"Where are you going?" came a querulous voice from inside.

"To get the boat ready. Just stay quiet, and you're as good as in Sweden."

He closed the door as Olaf joined us from the truck, and with Max in the lead the three of us made our way down a path to the beach. When we reached the water's edge I could see, far to the south, a faint glow that might have been the lights of Landskrona, a dozen or more miles away, and to the north was a similar glow that probably marked Hälsingborg, across from Elsinore; but directly ahead the Sound was black and unwelcoming, and a chill wind whipped little waves onto the beach at our feet. The island of Hven was somewhere out in the blackness. I looked at the stars overhead, wondering how I would ever remember the North Star once Max had pointed it out to me, and took some faint comfort in the fact that I could use the glow of the distant lights as a guide. How I would get back had not yet occurred to me.

Max pointed his light at the sand and blinked it once, then twice, then once again, and in a moment there was an answering blink from the bushes to our left. We went toward it, and a man rose up and approached us.

"Where's the boat?" Max asked.

"The Gestapo impounded it. They've got it under guard."

There was a short silence before Max said, "What about another?"

"We're looking now. It may take a while."

"It can't take too long. We're got thirty-five people here; either we get them across tonight, or we've got to find a place for them."

"I know. We're doing the best we can."

Max took a deep breath, and let it out slowly. "And those children," he said. "Once they start waking up . . ." He turned to Olaf. "You don't by any chance have any snaps on you, do you?"

"Don't I wish I did," Olaf replied.

"I don't mean for us; I mean for the children. That's the only thing to quiet 'em if they start crying."

"You want a bunch of drunken children on your hands?" said the other man.

"Better than a bunch of dead ones," Max replied.

"Well, it's academic anyway," said Olaf. "I don't even have a beer. . . . Wait a minute. There are some kegs in the truck, for camouflage. I wonder if they're empties."

"Why not look and see?" said Max. "It'd be better than nothing."

Olaf disappeared up the path, and Max and the other man and I stood by the water, listening for any sound of a boat engine. But all we heard was the slap of the waves on the beach, until suddenly the man grabbed my arm, said, "Quick! Into the bushes!" and ran. Max and I followed him, and tried to burrow into the underbrush without making too much noise. I had no idea what we were hiding from until I heard a clink of metal and the sound of boots in the sand, and then a German patrol came past. There were four of them, armed and helmeted, and they were making the small talk of soldiers who have nothing else to think about.

"This would be a good place to take a girl for a picnic," one of them was saying. "Have a little swim, then a beer while you're drying off, then into the bushes for a while— man, this occupation duty wouldn't be half bad if you played it right."

"If you could find a girl to come with you," another said. "I haven't found a Danish broad yet who'd so much as look at me."

"You don't go about it right," said the first, and then they were past, and their voices faded. We had drawn our pistols, just in case, and now we returned them to our belts.

"They'll be back," our man said, when they were out of hearing.

"When?" Max asked.

"It all depends how far they go. I didn't expect them this soon."

Max laughed. "That's all we need." He stood up as Olaf came down the path from the truck. "That was nice timing," Max said. "A little quicker, and you'd have walked right into a German patrol."

"I was testing the beer," Olaf said. "I had to show them how to do it."

"Well, that's not the final answer. We've got to get them out of here."

"Tell me something new. Which way'd the patrol go?"

"South. They'll probably be back."

"How many?"

"Four."

"I've got a Sten gun in the truck. We could set up a little ambush."

"Let's not if we don't have to. The less noise we make, the better."

We were quiet for a few moments, then Max said, "How are the adults?"

"Nervous," Olaf replied.

"Noisy nervous?"

"Not yet."

Max looked out at the black water. *"Damn,"* he said. "There's got to be a boat around here somewhere!"

"There are plenty of boats," the other man replied. "It's just a matter of getting them into the water."

I don't know how long we waited, but it seemed like hours. With one ear we were listening for a boat, and with the other for the return of the patrol, and all the time we were listening for the sound of children crying. There was nothing to do except wait, and I'd never realized what a strain that can be. If you can believe it my neck muscles ached from listening, and I was beginning to get a headache. Then the man, who clearly had better hearing than the rest of us, put up his hand.

"There!" he said. "There's a boat!" We listened even harder, and faintly, from the north, came the chugging of an engine. It grew louder, and the man stepped to the water's edge and blinked his light twice. He waited about a minute, blinked again, and then stepped back. "He got it," he said. "He's coming toward us."

Slowly, out of the darkness, a shape began to take form, but it wasn't until it got close that I could see it was two boats, one towing the other. The first was a squat-shaped fishing boat with a small cabin, and what it was towing looked like a launch, long and thin and low in the water. The boatman cut his engine and drifted toward shore, and we waded out to hold him from coming completely aground.

"What took you so long?" our man said.

The boatman's answer was a short laugh.

"All right, let's do this fast," Max said. "Louis, you get the people from the hearse and take them in the launch, and Olaf, you bring those from the truck and we'll put them in the fishing boat." As an afterthought he added, "You might bring your Sten gun, too."

"I had that in mind," Olaf replied, as we hurried up the path.

By the time we came back, herding the frightened, stumbling people onto the beach, the launch had been detached from the fishing boat and its engine started, and our man was holding the gunwale. The people clambered in, splashing and slipping and moaning and handing the unconscious children from one to another, and then I climbed aboard and got behind the wheel. I fumbled for the controls but didn't know what I was looking for, and had to ask the man for his flashlight. He showed me the direction lever and the throttle, then shoved the boat off from the beach, and I was on my own.

Hesitantly I pushed the lever forward; the engine noise changed from chugging to grinding, and we began to move. I headed out, away from the shore, and started a wide circle. This was partly to get used to the launch, and partly because I wanted the fishing boat to go ahead and let me follow. Only then did I remember I'd forgotten to ask Max about the North Star.

It seemed to take the fishing boat a long time to load, but finally I heard its engine and saw it coming out from the shore, and I swung in behind and adjusted my speed to follow. From the feel of my launch I guessed it had more speed than the other, but I was in no hurry to lead the way in that darkness, and decided I'd save the speed for when I might need it. This, I came to see later, was what saved me that night.

For anyone who's never done it, running a boat at night is an experience like none other in the world. Dark shapes appear and disappear and change; the line between land and water is virtually nonexistent, and a light that seems fairly close can be miles away—and what seems like a distant light can be right on you. There is no aid except experience, and for the inexperienced it can be a confusing and terrifying thing. There is a tendency to go in circles, and unless the boat's wake is phosphorescent you can't tell if you're on a straight course or not. The only way I kept on an even semi-straight track was by following the loom of the fishing boat ahead of me, and even then I sometimes lost it and began to wander. Once I thought I heard the sound of firing behind us, but when I looked back I couldn't see anything, and it was some time before I could find the fishing boat again. I finally located it by crossing its wake and then running up it.

I don't know how far we'd come, but it must have been two or three miles, when suddenly a white beam split the night ahead, and I saw the fishing boat lit up in the glare of a spotlight. I swung hard left, away from the light, and crept into the comforting darkness. Slowly I increased my speed, circling behind the German patrol boat as it closed in on the fishing boat, and when they were both behind me I opened the throttle wide, and the boat surged under me. The last time I looked astern the German boat had made contact, and its men were boarding the fishing boat. The people in my boat began to moan, and some to wail. The children, mercifully, stayed quiet.

By now I could make out the shape of Hven, and as the boat raced toward it over the black water I felt an exhilaration I'd never known before. We seemed almost to be flying, the waves slapping our bottom as we skipped along, and when we rounded the northern end of the island and were safely in Swedish waters, I let out a whoop of delight. There was no answering cheer behind me, and I wondered how many of them had friends or relatives on the fishing boat.

The lights of Landskrona were clear and bright now, and I headed for them. I'd forgotten, after three and a half years of blackout, how beautiful lights look at night, and they have a special magic when you're approaching them from the sea. I found myself envying the people in my boat, thinking they were to live in this marvelous wonderland of lights, and when I tied up at the nearest pier I had a sudden, insane urge to go ashore with them, if only for a little while.

There was someone at the pier to direct them—the Swedes had set up an efficient reception organization—and the last I saw of them they were walking in a ragged file into the city, too stunned to be aware of their surroundings. I headed back toward the darkness of Denmark, feeling for the first time that I'd accomplished something positive, and worth doing. It made me feel so good I was almost ashamed, because compared to what other people were doing it was nothing.

The trip back was confusion of the highest order. The boat,

it turned out, did have a compass, but the switch that turned on the compass light also turned on the running lights, and I didn't want to advertise my passage any more than necessary. Also, I didn't know how to steer an accurate course, and furthermore didn't know what course to set because I didn't have a chart, so I decided not to worry about seamanship, and to grope my way instead.

And grope I did. From Hven I headed for what I guessed was the Rungsted part of the coast, and tried by looking at the stars to head in a constant direction, but it was a long time before I saw the loom of land ahead, and when I did I couldn't recognize anything. From the length of time it took I thought I might have come too far to the south, so I headed north, and soon found myself seeing lights that could only mean I was headed back for Sweden. I circled around, keeping the lights astern, and after another stretch of time I couldn't see anything. The stars seemed to have changed, and I couldn't find those I'd been using as guides. I continued on, flicking the lights every now and then to check my compass heading, and the farther I went, the farther I seemed to get from everything. Finally a German patrol boat caught me in his spotlight, and I was almost relieved when he hailed me and came alongside.

"Where do you think you're going?" came a voice from the darkness behind the light.

"I wish I could tell you," I replied. "I'm lost."

The boat bumped beside mine, and I could faintly see a machine gun pointed at my face. I felt naked in the glare, but I knew they couldn't prove anything so I wasn't too worried.

"What are you doing out here, anyway?" the voice asked.

"Fishing," I replied.

"That's no fishing boat."

"Don't I know it. Some bastard stole mine."

"What kind did you have?"

I gave him, as clearly as I could remember, a description of the fishing boat I'd started out with, and concluded, "They probably turned it into a lousy Jew boat."

There was a silence, and then he said, "Where you headed for?"

"Rungsted."

"Boy, you're way off. You're coming up on Saltholm."

"*Saltholm?*" This was an island below Copenhagen, twenty miles south of where I wanted to be!

"That's right. You'd better do something about your compass."

With that he threw his engines into gear and roared off, leaving me rocking in his wake. The sky was beginning to turn gray in the east when I finally groped my way up the coast to Rungsted, and I eased into the boat basin and tied up at the first empty slip. Not knowing what else to do I made for the shore road, and started walking back to Copenhagen. A farmer in a horsecart picked me up after a while, and I slept the rest of the way into town.

Not every trip was as fouled up as that one, and I wasn't always the boatman. Sometimes I was a driver, sometimes a decoy, and sometimes little more than a messenger. But I always liked it when I got to run a boat, and I even began to think of having one of my own after the war. There was a sense of freedom about running a boat, and a clean and zesty feeling you don't get many other places.

Once or twice I worked with Ole, who was apparently getting his assignments from a contact other than mine, and once I was the guide who took a group from Bispebjerg Hospital to the embarkation point. I waited on a wooded stretch of road for the spot where I was to pick them up, and when I saw the truck coming I gave the prearranged signal; the truck flashed the reply and slowed down enough for me to jump aboard. I swung into the cab and said, "Keep going straight until I tell you," and the driver laughed. "What's funny?" I asked.

"Hello, Jens," my father said.

I was stunned for a second, then we both laughed.

"I guess sooner or later it was bound to happen," I said. "How do you like your work?"

"I'll tell you something," he replied. "I've never felt so good in my life. I hate to have it happen at someone else's expense, but for the first time that I can remember, I'm doing something important. And I don't mean to make it sound *self*-important—this is just something that must be done, no more and no less, but it gives me a wonderful lift to be doing it. Does that make any sense to you?"

"It certainly does," I replied. "I think a lot of people feel that way."

He thought for a moment, then said, "Well, I feel reborn, I can tell you that. You know what those swine did today?"

"You mean the Germans? Take a right here—right by this tree."

"Yes, the Germans. They had one of their so-called clearing murders at the hospital. I don't know why they call them clearing murders, unless they think it clears the air. At any rate, they—"

"Bear left here."

"—they suspected we were hiding Jews by disguising them as patients, so a bunch of Gestapo gunners came in during an operation and wiped out the whole O.R.—patient, doctors, nurses—everybody. Just gunned them all to pieces. Now, what kind of a madman does it take to do a thing like that?"

"I don't know," I replied. "I really don't know."

"When I think how I tried to understand them in the beginning—it's a wonder your mother and you are speaking to me."

"Well, they're not all like the Gestapo."

"As far as I'm concerned they are."

"Now stop here, and wait for a light. No, they're not. If it weren't for the Army, we wouldn't be getting away with all this."

"What do you mean?"

"The professional Army, the old-line Prussians, think this thing stinks. They say their soldiers have better things to do than harry a bunch of helpless civilians, and time and again they've simply looked the other way. If they'd chosen to bear down on us, we'd have been murdered. Did you see that light?"

"I just saw a blink in the bushes."

"That was it. Drive toward it."

"Well, for my money they're all Gestapo, and they can all roast in hell. Now what do I do?"

"Wait a minute, and the bushes will be taken away." As I spoke the bushes began to move, and in a minute or so the way was clear to the beach. My father eased the truck forward until I told him to stop, and then the bushes were replaced behind us. In front of us lay the Sound, and the distant glow of Sweden. A boat lay waiting at a small wooden pier, and I wished I were going along.

"All right," I said, opening the door on my side. "You can let the passengers out. And if you see Mother before I do, give her a kiss for me."

"I'll do that. Oh, by the way—"He lowered his voice "—I may have another volunteer."

"Great," I said. "Who?"

"Hans Bjøl. Whom do I tell?"

"Mr. Bjøl?" I felt a strange prickle on my skin. "Tell your contact."

"I don't really have a contact. I'm just a driver."

"Well—how much have you told him?"

"Nothing. Just if he was interested in helping, I thought I could find a way."

"You shouldn't have said that."

"Why not? I didn't tell him anything."

"Except that you're in the underground."

"Nothing of the sort. I just said I thought I might find a way."

"That was too much."

"Well, if he wants to help, I don't see the harm."

"No, I suppose not. I'll talk to someone and let you know."

"All right. Thank you for the pathfinding." He opened his door and got out, and I sat for almost a minute, nursing my feeling of foreboding. Then I went down and joined the others on the beach.

Chapter Twelve

They got him a week later, in an ambush. I talked to a man who survived the affair, and he told me that the Germans had been waiting on the beach, and held their fire until the people were strung out in a long line, getting into the boat. Then they simply cut them down. He escaped by jumping into the water and waiting until it was all over, and he said he saw them haul my father out of the truck and take him away. As to whether or not he was alive the man couldn't say, but the fact that they took him away was a good sign. If you could call a thing like that good; they clearly wanted to save him for interrogation, and that was something I tried not to think about. My father's life hadn't been the kind to prepare him for much torture.

I tried to think how best to break this to my mother, and could find no alternative to the plain facts. If he survived the interrogation he would probably be taken to Vestre prison, an ugly, dirty yellow building in the southwest part of the city; then to Horserød camp, in north Sealand; then possibly to a concentration camp in Germany. That was the routine, and we would probably be able to communicate with him through the underground somewhere along the way. Always providing, of course, he survived the interrogation, which would take place either in Shell House or in Dagmar House. No matter how you looked at it, his future was bleak.

My mother was in a state of wild excitement when I got home. "Oh, God, I'm glad you're here!" she cried, throwing her arms around me. "How did you know I needed you?"

"Then you've heard?" I said.

"Heard—I almost walked into it! Your father hasn't been home in two days, and just this morning I—"

"That's what I meant. He was caught by the Germans."

She stopped, and her eyes widened. "Oh, no," she said, in a small voice. "I was afraid of it, but—where is he? Did they hurt him?"

I told her all I knew, and when I was done she sank into a chair. "Well, we still have hope," she said. "At least they didn't take that away from us."

"That's right. Now, what were you going to tell me about you?"

"It doesn't seem so important now. It was just a near miss."

"Tell me anyway."

"Well—I suppose you know what Mrs. Jørgensen and I were doing."

"I have no idea."

"I thought you must know everything. We were making grenade fuses."

"Where?"

"In their basement. Mr. Jørgensen had a workshop, where he made all sorts of things."

"So?"

"So I used to go there every day when my housework was done and Lise and I would pass the time of day while we made fuses. It was nice, because we felt we were contributing something. Not much, but something." Her voice had a dreamy, faraway quality.

"But what *happened*?"

"This morning I was worried about your father, so I stayed around the house later than usual. Then, when I'd still heard nothing, I decided to go over to the Jørgensens', just to keep my mind occupied. As I approached their house I saw this big lorry outside, and then out came these two Germans with Lise between them. She gave me one look and then pretended not to see me, and I walked straight on past as though she weren't there. But that look on her face will haunt me as long as I live."

"What about Mr. Jørgensen?"

She shrugged. "I presume they got him, too. One glance at his basement, and they'd know everything."

I thought for a moment, then said, "Who else knew about this?"

"Nobody. Oh—Mrs. Bjøl."

"Mrs. *Bjøl*?"

"Yes. She'd noticed I was at the house a lot, and one day she asked Lise if she had a sewing circle or what, and Lise said in a manner of speaking, yes. She asked if she could join, and Lise wasn't too keen about it but she finally agreed. I suppose she must have blabbed."

"I suppose so. Did she ever join?"

"She came once."

"When?"

"A couple of days ago."

So there it was. On the circumstantial evidence, both Mr. and Mrs. Bjøl were informers. The case against her was much stronger than against him, but at the very least they should both be put under observation. I made an appointment to meet Stig at Tivoli that afternoon, and as we rode the roundabout I told him what I knew.

"We'll put a tail on them," he said, when I was through. "And don't let your mother—my God!" He suddenly sat bolt upright. "How come they didn't get your mother, too?"

"She kept walking past."

"But if Mrs. Bjøl informed, she'd have given your mother's name as well."

I suddenly felt cold all over. "Well, she was away from the house for a while," I said. "But then she came back—"

"When was this?"

"This morning."

"You get back to the house this minute, and tell your mother to go in hiding. If she has a friend she can go to, fine; if she doesn't we'll arrange something. Get moving."

I all but flew off the roundabout, and on my way out of the park collided with Holger Andersen, who was coming in.

"Going somewhere?" he asked.

"Sorry, Holger, I've got to hurry," I said, moving past. "What's the rush?"

"I just remembered I left a cake in the oven. Talk to you later." And with that I set off down the street, going as fast as I could without attracting attention.

I don't think any trip I've ever made took as long as that one. I knew every house and every paving block along the way, and each one took an interminable time to pass. I knew I shouldn't hurry too fast but I couldn't force myself to go slowly, and I was in that dream state where you run and run and get nowhere. When at last I turned down our street I was prepared to see the German lorry in front of our house, and when it wasn't there I was so relieved I almost missed the importance of the Volkswagen parked across the street. As I approached I could see there was one man sitting in it, reading a newspaper with the heavy-handed nonchalance that only a Gestapo man could affect, and I kept on walking as though he didn't exist. I went the length of the street and turned the corner, then crossed the avenue and took a position where I could see without being seen. I settled down to wait and try to think of what to do.

Two things were clear: One, my mother wasn't home, and two, they hadn't caught her, or they wouldn't be watching the house. (The fact that it was definitely she they were after was established when another Gestapo man came out of our house, talked to the man in the Volkswagen, and then went back inside.) But was she away because she knew they were after her, or had she gone off on some errand, and might she return any minute? And in the latter case, how could I warn her? She'd most likely enter the street from the other end, as I had, but that would depend on what area she was coming from, and that was one of the things I had no way of knowing. All I could do was stay put for the time being and, if I saw her coming from the other end, try to get the word to her in time.

I waited until it got dark, and when it was clear she wasn't coming back I left, wishing the Gestapo men a happy night's vigil. It appeared she'd either been warned, or on her own had realized she was in danger, and had vanished. All that remained for me was to find her. It was lucky I was able to stay at the University, because for the moment I had no home. It was dark and empty and full of memories, and no place for me at the moment. It would stink of Gestapo for a long time.

I saw Stig next day, this time at Langelinie, where the Little Mermaid sits on her rock at the harbor edge. It had Tivoli's advantage of being a place where many people go, and it didn't have Tivoli's disadvantage of apparently being a hangout for Holger Andersen. Having run into him twice

I was just as glad to avoid the place; I didn't know what he was doing, but I didn't want to give him a chance to see me too often. Many of the Schalburg Corps were being used as undercover men by the Gestapo, and until I knew more about him I preferred to avoid him.

As Stig and I strolled along the walk we pretended to watch the white clouds piling up like snowfields to the north, and I told him about the Gestapo watch on my house. Among other things it confirmed Mrs. Bjøl as the informer, and when I told Stig he nodded.

"He's one, too," he said. "We put a tail on him. He reports direct to Dagmar House."

"Oh," I said, thinking of my father's offer to enlist him. "What are you going to do?"

Stig glanced at me. "You guess."

I had a funny feeling in my stomach.

"I hope they weren't good friends," he said.

"Why?"

"It's just messier if they were."

"Well, they weren't." I remembered my father's saying he wouldn't have Mrs. Bjøl in the house, and wished he'd been a little stronger about her. I thought of the Bjøls, both of them plump when everyone else was thin, and wondered if they'd been getting extra ration stamps for their services. I thought of a lot of things, including Mr. Bjøl's assertion that the Allies had already won the war, and I concluded you can't tell a man from the way he talks. It occurred to me he probably took that line as a cover-up, or to sound out other people's feelings. Well, you live and you learn, I told myself. And if you don't learn, you often don't live.

We then got onto the matter of where my mother could be. Stig asked about friends with whom she might be staying, but I was no help there because the only people I could think of were the Jørgensens, who at this point were probably in

Shell House, or Dagmar House, or wherever.

"Well, I'll put someone on it," he said. "I don't imagine she's gone very far. Oh—incidentally, your father is in Vestre."

"How is he?" I asked, not really wanting to know.

"All right, I gather. It didn't take them long to find out he knew nothing."

It didn't take them long. I wondered how long it seemed to him, while they were doing things to him with cigarettes and hoses and blackjacks and the like, and although I tried to put the picture out of my mind I couldn't quite succeed. "Is there any chance of getting him out?" I asked.

"I doubt it. We'll have to see."

And with that we parted, he to wherever his business took him, and I to the offices of *Politiken,* the paper my father had worked on, to see about a part-time job. For all practical purposes I was an orphan, and I needed money. It's a weird feeling, to have parents who are alive but cut off from you and invisible; it's almost as though they were dead and you're dreaming about them, and I'm here to state it's one of the loneliest feelings in the world.

I got a job, as a copyboy in the city room, and one of the first news items I handled told how Mr. and Mrs. Hans Bjøl, of Høyensgade 17, had been found in their blood-spattered living room, apparently the victims of underground executioners. A rapid-fire gun of some sort had been used, because there were bullets in the floor, the walls, and the furniture, and on the door was pinned a note: "Landlord—sorry about the bullet holes."

There was a rule, imposed by the Germans, that news of the execution of informers could receive no more and no less space than the execution of saboteurs, so the Bjøls' first and last appearance in print ran alongside that of a boy from Aarhus who'd derailed a German munitions train in Jutland.

Until September of that year the Germans had been reluctant to execute Danish subjects, but the sabotage grew at such a rate that they finally started, and by November the death penalty for sabotage was a certainty. One additional item, anent the equal-space rule: A saboteur and a factory guard killed each other one night, and their deaths were given equal space, as required. But when they were buried, thirty people went to the guard's grave, and ten thousand followed the saboteur's coffin to the cemetery.

By the end of October, all but four hundred and seventy-two of the approximately seven thousand Jews had been transported to Sweden, and the underground developed a muscle it had never known before. The routes set up for the Jews were later used for escaping saboteurs and downed Allied fliers, and the vast majority of the population stood ready to assist in any way it could. It's been estimated that the Resistance grew to forty thousand people, and while forty thousand might have *helped* the Resistance, there were no more than four thousand active, dedicated workers, under the strict control of the Freedom Council. There were six main fields:

1. Sabotage, both railroad and factory.
2. Executions (in all, a hundred and seventy collaborators and informers were liquidated).
3. Arms drops.
4. Underground papers.
5. Harassment.
6. Radio transmission.

The last item I haven't touched on because I had no part in it, but it was one of the most important and certainly the most dangerous of all. In late 1941 or early 1942 the British dropped the first radio transmitter, to establish contact with the underground, and while it worked fairly well it was too bulky to be practical. Working with it as a starter, the Danes developed smaller and smaller models until they came up with the so-called "telephone book" version, which was the size its name implies and could be easily transported and hidden. The importance of being able to get messages out was obvious: The British had to know what our needs were, what drops had or had not succeeded, and what the general situation was at any given time. The dangers of transmission were that the German direction finders would pick up the signal the minute it was sent out, and the operator had just so much time to send his message, dismantle his set, and be someplace else by the time the Germans arrived. Furthermore, the higher up he was the better distance he got, but that also made him more vulnerable to capture. A church steeple, for instance, was an ideal sending spot except for the fact that it's a long way down, and if the church was suddenly surrounded, the operator had had it. Thus the preferred spot was a place like a block of apartments, high up and with lots of doors leading from one flat to another, thereby giving multiple choices for escape. You could move around a block of flats fairly handily—always providing there were no informers to turn you in. As I said, it was a dangerous business, and the casualty rate among telegraphers was higher than in any other line. They weren't executed, as were saboteurs, but they were packed off to jail for the duration. And many were killed in the process of being arrested.

One other item, which I wasn't aware of until I went to work at the newspaper, was the existence of *Information*, an underground news service. It had started sometime in August, when Børge Outze, a crime reporter and subeditor on the newspaper *Nationaltidende*, struck on a way to use all the news items that crossed his desk but were unprintable because of German regulations. (What the Germans would and would not allow is too complicated to go into here.) He started slipping these items to friends on underground papers, and they became so popular that he was finally persuaded to put out a daily bulletin, headed "For Information." It was a simple recitation of facts, without editorializing, and it finally burgeoned into a full-fledged clandestine news service. Outze was betrayed by an informer and jailed, but the work was carried on by others, and at the end of the war *Information* was supplying a daily, reasonably complete picture of life in Denmark not only to the underground papers, but also to the outside press (via Sweden), the BBC, the overseas Danish broadcast services, and the world in general. It surfaced after the war and became a successful daily newspaper.

I've gone into all this detail about underground activities to show how diverse they were, and how much there was to be done after the rescue of the Jews. Generally speaking, people took one branch of work and stayed with it, but sometimes the demand was such in another branch that you'd move out of your specialty for a while, and give help where it was needed. Most of the time after October I was assigned to sabotage, which was becoming the number one activity. Ole, I found out, was in harassment, where his particular genius was extremely useful—while it lasted.

Now we should go back for a moment, to a few days after my mother's disappearance. Stig had said he'd find her, and I had no doubt he would, and I had a couple of trips to Sweden that kept me from doing any searching on my own. I won't say I wasn't worried, but I had such confidence in Stig that I felt sure she'd be all right, and that if she wasn't I'd be the first to know. It's good to work with a group like that, whose lives are interdependent one on the other, and it's a feeling that doesn't, sad to say, come often in peacetime.

I was at the University this day, trying to keep at least the pretense of being a student, when Ole came up to me after one of my classes. With a grin that split his silly face, he said, "Guess where your mother is."

"Where?" I said.

"Guess."

"I can't. Tell me."

"Take just one guess."

"Damn it, Ole, will you cut it out? Where is she?"

"At Uncle Mogens'."

"Are you sure?"

"That's where I saw her. She asked me to tell you."

"Is she living there?"

"So I gather. Uncle Mogens says it's the greatest thing since the invention of gunpowder."

"What is?"

"Having someone to talk to. He says he's tired of telling his ideas to watches."

I looked at the clock. I still had an hour before I was due at the paper, so I thanked Ole and set off for Uncle Mogens'. He opened the door almost before I'd had a chance to knock, and as he let me in he said, "I thought this might get you here. Where've you been keeping yourself?"

"Here and there." I had the brief, horrible thought that this might have been a ruse to get me to come, but then she came out of the back room, and we were hugging and kissing and weeping like a pair of long-lost lovers. In front of anyone else I'd have been embarrassed, but I felt that Uncle Mogens was part of the family.

When, finally, we could talk, we sat in the back room and Uncle Mogens brought out three bottles of beer, and we caught up on things. It turned out she'd slowly realized, that day, the same thing that came to Stig on the roundabout: that her name had probably been turned in with the Jørgensens'. So she left, not knowing exactly what to do, and on her way down the street she passed the Volkswagen as it arrived, and she saw it stop across from the house. She didn't wait to see more; she came straight to Uncle Mogens (with whom, it turned out, she'd been in contact through her grenade fuses) and told him the story, and he took her in. I said I hadn't been back to the house since that first day, and we both agreed it was a place to stay away from for a while, although she said she desperately needed clothes and various personal effects, and it was clear that I could do with a change myself. We decided that if we could both hold out for another day or so, I'd go back some night and pack up what I could. I didn't think the Gestapo would keep a watch on an empty house for more than a week.

After that I had to go, but I can tell you I was a different person from the one who walked into the newspaper office the first time. Then the world had seemed hollow and empty and awful, and now there was hope. And without hope, believe me, there's no point in anything. But with it, even the smallest sliver of it, you can knock the tops off mountains. That may sound trite and obvious, but if you've ever felt the difference you'll know there's more to it than just the words.

Chapter Thirteen

Kaj Munk was murdered that winter. On Tuesday, January 4, 1944, the poet, preacher, and "greatest dramatist of the north since Ibsen" was dragged from his vicarage in west Jutland by four men, shot several times, and left in a ditch near Silkeborg, General von Hanneken's headquarters. The papers were required to print his obit the same size as that of a fishmonger informer who'd been liquidated the same day. The Germans tried to make it appear that Munk had been working for them, and had therefore been done in by the underground, but that ploy was short-circuited when a writer and member of the underground jumped on the stage of the Opera House in Copenhagen and shouted, "They're trying to say we killed him, but it was they who killed him—we loved him!" He then blew a kiss to the audience and vanished into the wings.

My duties that winter included learning the gentle art of sabotage, and believe me that's something you learn quickly or you can forget the whole thing. I once saw a bicycle rider in the circus who came down a long ramp and then took off and did a somersault in the air, bicycle and all, and it occurred to me to wonder how you practiced such a thing; you either did it right the first time or you spent the rest of your life in a cast. Learning sabotage was somewhat the same; you'd better do it right very early on.

A saboteur, in case you hadn't guessed it, led a strange and different life. He couldn't sleep between four thirty and six AM, because that was when the Germans liked to pick people up and get them to make the wrong answers while they were still half asleep. He had to suspect everybody, especially people whose habits changed in the slightest or who seemed either too pro- or too anti-British. If they were too blasé it was a bad sign, just as it was if they were too emotional. He had to try always to maintain his own habit pattern, for fear of giving himself away to people who were watching him. It was a vicious circle; everyone was suspicious of everyone else—except, of course, those they knew to be on their side —and it often turned out that those who acted the least suspiciously were those to be trusted the least. It was like living on the rim of a lighted pinwheel.

The handling of explosives was an art all its own. The PE#2, plastic explosives were safe enough to work with, but they exuded a sweet, almondy smell like marzipan, which got in your clothes and made you reek like a candy store for hours afterward. And nitroglycerin, otherwise known as 808, was a more powerful but also more volatile explosive, and if you handled it without gloves, or without coating your hands with vaseline, it got into your pores and gave you a a headache as bad as the explosion it caused. As a matter of fact both PE and 808 could give you a headache if you used them bare-handed, but the 808 made you wish you'd left your head behind.

And there were all different kinds of fuses, too: some the standard, wick type; some electrically detonated, or by percussion cap; and some made out of slow-burning materials like pressed coke. These latter had an interesting feature in that their burning time varied with the temperature of the air; one time we planted PE in a factory and lit the fuse and never did hear the explosion, because the night was so cold it took several hours for the thing to go off. When it did we were in our various beds, stinking of marzipan and trying to pretend we'd been asleep all night. The factory guards, naturally, weren't going to go snooping around after we'd left, because they didn't know any better than we when to expect the explosion. When they finally untied themselves, they simply called it an evening and went home. They may have been slobs, but they weren't stupid. (In all fairness to them there was a problem of unemployment, and many people who would have preferred not to work for the Germans were forced to, simply to feed their families.)

As winter wore on and spring came near, there were growing signs that the Allies were about to invade the Continent, and this spurred the sabotage even further. The Freedom Council wanted to be prepared to act in concert with the Allies when they invaded, to have a military force that could work from behind the German lines, and to that end they didn't want any of the underground to expose themselves prematurely. Any damage to the German war effort was, of course, to be encouraged; the only thing the Council discouraged was senseless rioting that did nothing but get people killed. The members of the underground obeyed, but the people had been held down too long to have patience any longer. The Germans, naturally, put this impatience to their own use. By the end, they were inciting riots as an excuse to shoot people down.

One day in May, when the air smelled of spring, Ole came to the newspaper as I was going to work. He had that look on his face that I recognized, and I wondered what was on his mind.

"What are you doing tonight?" he asked.

"Nothing I know of," I replied. "Why?"

"When do you get through here?"

"Eight."

"Want to have some fun?"

"What kind?" Knowing him, I didn't want to commit myself right away.

"I'll tell you later. Do you have a rifle?"

"No. Why?"

"That's all right. I'll get you one."

"What's this all *about*?"

"I said I'll tell you later. Meet me at Fiskerihaven at ten." Fiskerihaven was an area where fishing boats put in, on the southern part of the harbor near the gas works and the railroad tracks. It was as unlikely a place to use a rifle as any I could imagine.

"What are you going to do?" I asked. "Shoot yourself some fish?"

"Be there," he replied with a smile, and left.

I was there at ten, and at first I couldn't see anything except boats and barrels and masts and spars. Then out of the darkness came Ole, pushing a hot-dog-vender's wagon. Behind him was a man I didn't recognize.

"Greetings," Ole said. "Welcome to the Potting Club."

"Thanks," I replied. "Is it all right to ask what we're doing?"

"Of course. We're potting."

"What do you mean?"

"Potting Germans."

"Look, Ole," I said, "It's been a long day, and if it's all right with you I'd—"

"It's very simple," he said. "Observe." He opened the cover of the hot-dog wagon and produced three rifles, handing one to me and one to the other man, and an extra clip of cartridges for each. "Now, we station ourselves out on the pier, and wait. At ten twenty, a man is going to call the Gestapo and tell them there's a suspicious boat down at the dock here, and naturally they'll send someone to investigate. Did you see Gustav when you came?"

"Gustav who?" I replied.

"Never mind. He saw you. He blinked to tell us you were coming. Gustav is stationed up the line there, and when the Gestapo come he'll blink his light as many times as they have men, so we'll know what to look for. Then, when they come onto the pier, we just pick them off. Simple?"

"You must be crazy," I said.

"Not in the least. It's worked time and again." He laughed. "We did a nice variation the other night. We pinched some land mines, and planted them on a back road near Veksø. Then we called the Krauts and told them there'd been an airdrop there, and—whambo! They hit every mine. It was a beautiful sight."

"You mean you stayed around to watch?"

"Of course. Why not?"

"How many of you do this?"

He coughed. "Well, we used to have quite a few. As a matter of fact, you're someone's replacement tonight. He couldn't make it."

"Thanks for thinking of me," I said.

"You're welcome." He peered at the luminous dial on his watch. "Let's get ourselves set up here," he said. "We want to be settled in by the time our guests arrive."

We spread out along the pier, barricading ourselves behind barrels and crates. Each man had his own emplacement, apart from the others but still enough to be within speaking range.

"Hold your fire till I give the word," Ole said. "The main thing we have going is surprise, so we don't want to scatter our fire."

I heard the click of his working the bolt on his rifle, and I did the same, set the safety catch, and waited. I had a feeling of complete unreality, but no fear. Somewhere along the line I'd lost my capacity to be afraid.

Ole turned, and looked at the harbor behind him. "There's a ship sitting at a funny angle over there," he said. "Did you notice it—kind of low in the water?"

"No," I replied. "I haven't been down here recently."

"It was loading goods for Germany. Last week, I guess it was. We filled a truck with explosives, started the fuse, then aimed the truck at the dock and let her roll. She dumped into the water beside the ship, and for a while the Krauts thought it was just some dope who hadn't set his brakes. Then the load went off, and my! Sprang every rivet in that ship's hull. Riverts were flying around like bumblebees." He savored the memory, then said, "You're in the wrong line of work, Jens. You ought to be where the fun is."

"I have my fun," I replied.

"Maybe, but not like this. By the way—how's Ingrid?"

"Speaking of fun? I wouldn't know. I haven't seen her in a while."

"Don't let that one go. That's very special."

"I don't intend to let her go. It's just that other things keep cropping up."

"I know. The war. I wonder what we'll do when it's over."

"I'm going to get a boat."

"And do what?"

"I don't know. There should be lots of things."

"I'm going to—let's see—I'd like to invent something that would make it impossible to start any more wars."

"That would be a neat trick. How would it work?"

"Well—did you ever have a girl laugh when you were trying to make out?"

"I can't say I have."

"Let me tell you, it's murder. Here you're feeling all hot and masculine and she starts laughing, and there's not a bloody thing you can do. You're wiped out."

"So?"

"So if you could arrange it that everyone laughed at someone who wanted to start a war—I don't know. There are a few bugs to be worked out of it, but I think I'm on the track of something. It'll take more thinking."

I thought of Ingrid's remark about how athletic Ole was in his courtship, and I wondered if she was the one who'd laughed. I decided I didn't want to know, because it seemed an unfair advantage to know as much as I did.

"Hey," said the other man. "A light!"

We saw a flashlight wink on and off, and Ole began to count. "One—two—three—four—five—what is this?" Suddenly, the light began to flutter so fast we couldn't count it, and Ole scrambled to his feet. "Into the water!" he shouted, and we slung our rifles on our shoulders and dropped off the edge of the pier into the icy harbor. As we made our way around behind a fishing boat we heard the first of the Gestapo cars arrive, then another, and another, and the pier above our heads thudded with the sound of boots. "They must have brought the whole of Dagmar House," Ole whispered, through his chattering teeth.

"You and your bright ideas," I replied. "I suppose you call this being where the fun is."

"It's always worked before," he said. "You can't blame me if they overreacted."

I don't know how long we stayed in that water. It seemed like all night, but it was probably about two or three hours.

We could hear the Germans methodically searching the whole area, and when they came aboard the fishing boat we had to sink beneath the surface, holding our breaths for as long as we could, and try not to make too much noise as we came up to breathe. The cold feeling finally wore off and was replaced by a numbness that made it hard to hold onto anything, and I wondered if I'd be able to climb out of the water when they finally left. I was slowly congealing, and began to have the drowsy sensation I'd heard was the prelude to death by freezing. This thought woke me up, and I clenched and unclenched my hands to keep some semblance of circulation going. I could hear Ole's teeth chattering nearby, and an occasional snort from the other man, who was fighting off an urge to sneeze. It turned out he was sneezing under water, which I gather is no particular fun.

At long last, with a great deal of stamping and shouting and slamming of doors, they left, and when the noise of their cars had died away Ole said, "Let's give them a few more minutes. It'd be just like them to leave someone behind to sandbag us."

We waited, but it was easier now because we could move about a little more, and when ten or fifteen minutes had passed Ole began to grope his way along the bulkhead. "There's a ladder here somewhere," he said. "I saw it when I jumped in." He found it and went up, and I followed with the other man behind me. It wasn't easy, because we were so numb we could barely move, but we finally made it. We crouched on the pier, dripping and shivering, and peered into the darkness.

"Anybody see anything?" Ole asked.

"What's that thing over there?" I said, pointing.

Ole studied it for a moment, then said, "A freight car. There's a siding comes down from the railyards. Let's make for that first."

"What for?" I asked.

"For cover. Just in case. You think you can run?"

"I can try."

He looked at the other man. "OK?"

"Anything's better than staying here," the man replied in a clogged voice.

"All right. Jens, you go first. Ready?" I nodded, and he touched my shoulder and said, "Go!" and I took off.

It was hard at first, but then my legs limbered up and I began to put on speed. I heard Ole say, "Go!" again, and heard the pounding of the man's feet behind me, and then, when I was about halfway to the freight car, the darkness turned to white light. I was vaguely aware of a ripping burst from a machine pistol, then another, and the man behind me gasped, and by the time the third burst came I was around behind the freight car and racing up the tracks. Another line of cars appeared, and I ran until I saw one with an open door; I swung up and flung myself inside, and fumbled my way to one end and crouched down between two barrels of what smelled like fish manure. I unslung my rifle and pointed it toward the door.

But nobody came. I didn't even hear any sounds of pursuit, and after a while I forced myself to think about Ole. I'd been trying not to; I assumed the man behind me had been hit, but that was on the second burst. I didn't know what had happened to the first or the third. And until I knew, I couldn't leave. Taking a deep breath and mumbling a garbled form of prayer, I slipped out of the car and, with my rifle at the ready, crept back toward the pier.

I could see lights, and as I got closer they resolved into automobile headlights and a hand-held spotlight, which was playing back and forth about the area. On the ground in front of the automobile were two bodies, arranged neatly side by side, and even from a distance I could tell from the hair which one was Ole's. A man was bending over his feet, doing something I couldn't see, and the man with the light was playing it on the boom of a cargo hoist. Then the other straightened up, and with the rope he'd been tying to Ole's feet he dragged the two bodies to the cargo hoist, strung them up, then lifted the boom so they were hanging, head down, six feet off the ground. Then the two men returned to the car and there, standing in the full glare of the headlights, was Holger Andersen. He'd been putting a new clip in his machine pistol, and now he returned it to his belt, said something to the men, and one of them went back and lifted the boom a little higher.

All right, Holger, I thought. Now you've had it. I lay beneath a freight car, aimed carefully at Holger's chest, and squeezed the trigger. It wouldn't move. I squeezed again, then realized I'd never taken it off safety. I said one short, sharp word, flipped the safety catch, and by the time I had my eye to the sights again Holger was in the car, and the other men were following him. I rested my forehead on the gunstock, and cried.

There wasn't much I could do for Ole and the other man except cut them down, and then go back and tell Stig what had happened. He wasn't easy to find at that hour of the night, but I couldn't sleep until I'd told him, so I tried every place I could think of and finally, about two thirty AM, I tracked him to Sigvald's. They were sitting in the kitchen with a couple of bottles of beer, and when they saw me with my soggy clothes and my rifle, they were astounded.

"You mean you walked through the streets carrying that cannon?" Stig asked.

"I forgot I had it," I replied. "I'm not kidding, I really did."

"You're lucky you weren't shot," he said. "Sit down."

"You don't know how lucky I am," I replied, and while Sigvald got me a beer I told what had happened.

"Who is this Holger Andersen?" Stig asked, when I was through. "What does he look like?"

I told him, and he shook his head.

"Never seen him," he said. "You'll have to point him out. And, I would say, the sooner the better. You know where to find him?"

"I've seen him a couple of times at Tivoli," I replied. "I think he may be staked out there."

"All right. Can you get him to talk to you?"

I smiled. "I think so."

"Do that. And, to make sure of the identification, put your hand on his arm. We don't want to rub out some other friend by mistake."

A thought occurred to me. "Suppose he recognizes me from tonight."

"Do you think he will?"

"No," I said, without conviction. "The light was never on my face. He worked from the rear forward."

"Well, even if he does, no matter."

"Suppose he tries to arrest me."

It was Stig's turn to smile. "We'll see he doesn't get very far."

"OK. What time should I be there?"

"Can you make it by two?"

"I don't know why not. I just have to change my clothes."

"Try for some sleep, too. It's best to be alert for these things."

"I'll try."

I tried, but it was no good. I had to go home for my change of clothes, and after carefully checking the area for Gestapo I went into the dark and empty house. The familiar smells greeted me, but at the same time there was something different; it smelled of my mother's absence and also, I swear, of the Gestapo. It was a sort of rancid smell, combined with stale cigar smoke. I took a bath and a brisk rubdown, then put on clean underwear and lay on the bed, but I couldn't sleep. No matter if my eyes were open or closed, I could still see Ole and the other man hanging from the cargo hoist, and I could hear the heavy, clattering thump when I cut them down. I finally got up, finished dressing, and left the house before daybreak.

I entered Tivoli at exactly two o'clock. It's an odd feeling to know you're being watched by someone, or possibly two people, unknown to you, and as my eyes wandered over the crowd searching for Holger I also looked for anyone who might be watching me. There were men, women, and children of all ages and sizes; there were girls in pairs and lone youths on the prowl; there were lovers walking hand in hand; and there was a faintly embarrassed man whose child had evidently gone to the public facilities, because he was holding a colored pinwheel on a stick and trying to pretend he wasn't. I felt sorry for him, and hoped the child would come back soon.

But nowhere did I see Holger. Then it occurred to me that if, as I suspected, the Gestapo had assigned him to watch Tivoli for suspicious characters, the best way to flush him out would be to act the part. So I drifted around the gardens acting suspiciously, and if you think that's easy you should try it some time. It couldn't be a parody of a furtive character; it had to be someone who was doing things just a little bit wrong. Since you're always supposed to act nonchalant, I acted a little too nonchalant; I whistled and snapped my fingers and looked at the sky, and I walked about in aimless circles as though waiting for an overdue contact. Then I remembered the tree in the park where I used to get my messages, and I decided to pretend that one of the trees in Tivoli was a message tree. I selected a tree and angled toward it, glancing once or twice back over my shoulder (which you're *never* supposed to do), and I casually, oh so casually, leaned against the tree and began to pick at the bark. Then, quickly, I put my hand in my pocket and started to walk toward the exit. Suddenly, in front of me, was Holger.

"Hi, there," he said.

"Well, *Holger!*" I replied, genuinely delighted. "Where've you been keeping yourself?"

"Here and there. Were you looking for someone?"

"No. Just taking the air. By the way, I want to apologize for the last time I saw you—" I leaned closer to him, and put my hand on his arm "—I said I'd left a cake in the oven, but that was a big fib." I began to laugh, and found I had difficulty stopping. All at once I was enjoying myself more than I had in years, and I wanted to prolong the game. It's a queer sensation to be looking into the eyes of someone who will shortly be dead, and I wanted to memorize every feature of his face so I could imagine what it looked like when they killed him. What with emotion and fatigue and everything I was probably a little unbalanced, and I found the whole thing exquisitely funny.

"What's the big joke?" Holger asked, as I continued to laugh.

"It's just that—" I put my hand on his arm again, to make sure the signal was caught "—just that I was really going to see a girl. I lied to you about the cake."

"I didn't think—" Holger began, but I wasn't listening.

"A Scout should never lie," I went on, trying to suppress my laughter. "A Scout is trustworthy, loyal, helpful, friendly, courteous, kind, obedient, cheerful, thrifty, brave, clean, and reverent. On my honor I will do my best to do my duty to God and my country, and to obey the Scout Law. To help other people at all times, and to keep myself physically strong, mentally awake, and morally straight, and to do a good turn every day. Amen."

Holger backed away from me. "Hansen, you're drunk," he said.

"Not in the least," I replied. "Just ebullient. And you know why? I got engaged today. You want to see the ring?" In case he still suspected me I decided to show him my pockets were empty, so I pretended to search for a ring, and in the process turned both pockets inside out and put their contents on the ground, all the while muttering, "I had it with me—I know I had it—son of a gun, where can it be?"

This was embarrassing for Holger because it drew attention, and he must have concluded I was either drunk or insane and in neither case on an underground mission, because he said, "Why don't you go home and sleep it off," and abruptly turned and walked away. As I was picking up my belongings from the ground I watched him leave, and saw the man with the child's pinwheel fall in behind him. The blades made a bright corkscrew of colors as they spun.

I saw Stig later that night, and the first thing he said was, "What were you doing, anyway? We didn't say you had to kiss the man."

"I didn't kiss him," I replied. "I just wanted to make sure they got the signal."

"They got it, all right."

"And did they get him?"

Stig looked at his watch. "As of now, he should be starting a halfway trip to Sweden."

"Why not shoot him on the spot?" I was afraid that, with the delay, he might have had a chance to escape.

Stig shook his head. "Not with the Gestapo," he said. "They'd have had a clearing murder right away—they'd have shot a dozen Danes on the spot where he was found. This way they won't find him, and they'll have to guess for a while."

"All right," I said. "So long as I know he's gone."

"He's gone," said Stig.

"I only wish I could have done it."

"Well, you can't have everything. You did your part."

"I guess you're right. And now, I think I'll probably sleep."

I did, for fourteen hours.

Chapter Fourteen

On June 6 an American, British, and Canadian force crossed the Channel and set up beachheads on the Normandy coast, and the joy in Denmark was unbounded. For obvious reasons there could be no overt celebrating, but for most of that day people had silly smiles on their faces, and here and there signs appeared, such as: "Learn English Before the English Get Here," all of which contributed to the general malaise of the Germans. They became sullen and nervous and trigger-happy; they put Danish hostages on their troop trains in Jutland in hope of deterring sabotage (a vain hope, as it turned out), and they instituted a campaign of counter-sabotage, wrecking Danish landmarks in reprisal for the factory bombings. For this work they used a gang of terrorists known as the Peter group, another clutch of thugs led by the Danish Nazi Henning Brøndum, and the ever-present Schalburg Corps. In all, they represented some of the lowest elements of German and

Danish society, and they accomplished little except to heighten the outrage of the people.

The sabotage and counter-sabotage grew at a wild pace in the weeks following the invasion, culminating in the so-called People's Strike at the end of the month. Just a few examples should give a general idea of the picture.

The first of the idiotic counter-bombings occurred when the Peter group destroyed the Pavilion of the Royal Yacht Club, an action they described as "a blow at the upper classes." These people were not only savage, they were stupid; it never occurred to them that by its very name the Royal Yacht Club was an extension of the King, who although virtually a prisoner was still the symbol of the Danish people. One way to answer these counter-bombings was with counter-counter-bombings, destroying the houses of known Nazis, but in the general climate of insanity that was only partially effective.

There were two successful sabotage actions on June 21, and although I took part in neither one the details were public knowledge in short order. In the first, fifty saboteurs bombed the Superphone Radio Factory, especially those sections where parts were being made for German rocket bombs, and got away unscathed. And here I'd like to add a side note: I mentioned earlier that military intelligence was one of the most important Danish contributions to the Allied cause, and the rocket business is an example. The first hint the British had of the German V-1 rocket came when an experimental model crashed on a Danish farm; the farmer called the police, and they came and photographed it in every detail and had its specifications in England before the Germans arrived to pick it up. That kind of intelligence service can be, to say the least, a great help.

The other action on the 21st was smaller, but no less successful. In this one, twelve saboteurs attacked the Bohnstedt-Petersen Motor Works in the Free Port, up by the Tuborg

Breweries. They planted their bombs and got away, but not before they'd had a running battle with the crew of a German gunboat, moored some fifty yards distant. Again the saboteurs suffered no casualties, although they came closer than they'd have liked. They hadn't counted on a gunboat's being part of the factory security system.

The next day, Thursday the 22nd, I took part in the largest single act of sabotage so far. We'd been preparing it for quite a while, which is why we weren't involved in the earlier actions, and our preparations paid off better than we could have hoped for in our wildest dreams. What we did was attack "the Scandinavian Krupp's," the third largest manufacturer of automatic weapons in Europe. Its legal name was Dansk Industrisyndikatet, otherwise known as Riffelsyndikatet, and a hundred of us armed with Sten guns arrived at its gates in the full daylight of six thirty PM, riding in a convoy of one ARP lorry, one ARP ambulance, and one regular lorry. I thought, as we joggled through the streets jammed together like paratroopers and clutching our Sten guns, of the days when Ole and I considered ourselves daring by putting sugar in the Germans' gas tanks, and I wished Ole were with me now.

The factory guards were so astounded when we swarmed in that they didn't put up even the pretense of a fight; they just raised their hands and let the men assigned to the job tie them up. I was one of those delegated to plant the explosives, and for the next little while I was so busy I didn't notice anything else that was going on. The main idea was to put the PE where it would do the most damage, either at a crucial spot in one of the machines or at a junction of the building beams, where it would weaken or destroy the structure when it went off. There was also some incendiary material, to insure a respectable fire after the explosions.

With my job finally done I joined the others at the entrance, and when everyone was clear of the building we started the fuses, got back in our lorries, and drove off. While some of us had been planting the explosives, another group had been loading the lorries with arms and ammunition, and the haul included seventy-two machine guns and a number of twenty-millimeter cannon. To say that the lorries were crowded would be an understatement. We stank of marzipan and perspiration, but we were as happy as schoolboys on a picnic. There was a great deal of laughter, most of it about things that weren't very funny.

After we were unloaded, I couldn't resist going back to see the results of our handiwork. It was a splendid fire, and it was burning out of control in spite of the presence of a great mass of fire-fighting equipment. Looking closely, I could see that the Germans were forcing the firemen at gunpoint to play the hoses on the flames, but the firemen were managing, through careful clumsiness, to have couplings come loose, nozzles malfunction, and in general do everything they could to nurse the fire along. It's not easy to be deliberately sloppy with a gun at your back, but they were doing quite well and I admired them.

The Riffelsyndikatet factory was next to the commuter railroad tracks, and when I saw a suburban electric train approaching I wondered it it was going to be able to get by. It did, at slow speed, and I could see the excited passengers crowding at the windows to watch the fire. Even above the other noises you could hear them cheering; the Germans also heard them, and whirled in a rage and fired into the train. The cheers turned to screams; bullet holes appeared in the windows, and the people fell back over one another. It developed later that only two were badly wounded—why, nobody was ever able to explain.

But the greatest triumph of the Riffelsyndikatet action, more satisfying even than the fire or the take in arms and ammunition, was the telegram of congratulations from General Eisenhower, in Supreme Headquarters, Allied Expeditionary Forces. That, plus General Montgomery's description of the Danish Resistance movement as "second to none," made up for a lot of the shame of the early years.

At this point I was living in the Studentergaarden, the the largest student residence in Copenhagen, and it was convenient because my comings and goings were unregulated and I could stay out all night if necessary. On the night after the Riffelsyndikatet I was asleep on my cot, catching up on three nights of little or no sleep, when I was awakened by the jarring thud of explosions, and then a slow, shattering crash mixed with shouts and screams, and the whole building collapsed around me. I rolled under my cot as a deluge of ceiling material came boiling down, and I waited in the dust and debris until the remains of the building had settled, and all that could be heard were the moans and cries of injured students. I spent most of the rest of the night helping with the survivors, and by the time everyone was accounted for we had two who were badly injured, and a number of others hurt in varying degrees. Why nobody was killed was a mystery like that of the commuter train; we could only assume that someone with a great deal of influence was on our side.

The Schalburg Corps were responsible for that bombing, as they were, the next night, for the fire in Tivoli that destroyed the Concert Hall and the Arena Dance Hall. A piece of raging stupidity like this is hard to explain; there were those who said that SS General Pancke had ordered it because people had been seen dancing the jitterbug and other decadent Anglo-Saxon numbers, but it was more likely that Werner Best ordered it, out of rage and frustration at the sabotage. The public outcry was such that Best, and even the Schalburg, denied any knowledge of the deed, but there was one witness who nailed the identity of the perpetrators beyond question. He was a night watchman, to whom one of the arsonists had said, "They think they know about sabotage—we'll show them what sabotage is really like." When asked who was "we," the reply came: "We of the Eastern Front." In other words, ex-Frikorps Schalburgers. Their other credits before they were disbanded were the bombing and/or destruction of the Langelinie Pavilion, the Klampenborg Golf Club, the hall of a Copenhagen sports club, the ARP building in Rosenvænget, the Domus Medica (headquarters of the Danish doctors' society), and the Royal Copenhagen Porcelain Works, to name only a few. It was hatred of the Schalburg Corps that played a leading part in the People's Strike, and the strike wasn't settled until the Germans agreed to take the Schalburgers off the streets.

There were two more bits of sabotage before the strike, and they were on Sunday the 25th, the day after the Tivoli fire. A group broke into Nordwerk, a German arms factory on Ryesgade, by blowing a hole in the street wall. They then placed their bombs inside, lit the fuses, and made off. The nearby Amdi factory, which made parts for airplane engines, was meanwhile being blown up by another group, and the two units got away after fighting off a patrol of German soldiers. It had now reached the point where the saboteurs could do pretty much as they wanted.

Best realized this, and in his desperation he announced a new set of rules, beginning Monday the 26th. No more than four people were allowed to meet in public streets or open places; meetings of any sort, indoors or out, were prohibited; the orders of German patrols were to be obeyed instantly and without question; and there would be a curfew from eight PM to six AM, stricter than that in occupied France.

That touched off the strike. The terms echoed those of August of 1943, but the curfew was more drastic, and it was taken as an insult. People treated it with the contempt it deserved, and went out as they pleased. To rub in the point they built bonfires in the streets, and defied the patrols who tried to break them up. The patrols opened fire, and in that first night seven Danes were killed and a number wounded. The challenge had been made, and accepted, and from then on both sides increased the pressure.

My part in all this was strictly as an observer, because the Freedom Council had ordered members of the underground to lie low, and not do anything that would reveal their identities to the Germans. The Germans, on the other hand, were doing everything they could to bring us into the open; they started all sorts of rumors (the English were in Norway, the Allies were in Holland, etc.) designed to force the underground into a premature uprising. But we didn't take the bait; we sat back and watched, and I must say it wasn't an easy role.

On Tuesday the 27th, the workers at Burmeister & Wain went home at two PM, explaining that, because of the curfew, they needed more time to tend their so-called allotment gardens. (These produced the desperately needed food to supplement the rationed items.) Their idea spread to other businesses, and next day saw the "home early" departure of all tram conductors and workers at General Motors, Atlas, Titan, and all bakeries, dairies, commercial offices, shops, and many large stores. That Wednesday night in the working-class district of Vesterbro, a man was shot in the back by the Schalburg; his wife ran screaming down the street, and an angry crowd gathered and began to mill around. In short order barricades were set up and bonfires lighted (old mattresses were very handy for bonfires), and gradually the rioting spread throughout the city. A riot is a strange and undefinable thing; nobody knows quite when it starts or what it is that starts it, but soon it begins to feed on itself, and what was a group of people talking to one another can turn into a howling mob.

It has been estimated that, in all, a thousand "freedom bonfires" were lighted that night. I saw one of them, in Nørre Voldgade, and it was a sight I shall never forget. The fire was burning in a pile of broken furniture, mattresses, and packing boxes, and perhaps fifty people were dancing a ring around it, holding hands and singing "Kong Christian," the Communist "Internationale," and "It's a Long Way to Tipperary." There were men and women, girls and boys, all circling and singing; the girls were dressed mostly in skirts and sweaters and the men were in jackets or shirtsleeves, but there was one woman—and I will never know who she was or where she came from—who was wearing a long white evening dress. The firelight played on her face and her dress, and I could see the sparkle of a necklace at her throat. Other people stood by and watched, some joining in the singing and some foraging extra fuel for the fire, and I was tempted to ignore instructions and join in the circle—after all, it wasn't a riot or anything like it—when from up the street came the stutter of gunfire and the smack and whine of ricocheting bullets; somebody screamed, and then there was another burst of gunfire and the crowd broke and scattered. As I ducked into a doorway I saw two people on the ground, one lying still and the other kicking. I saw no sign of the long white dress.

On Thursday we read how the village of Hvidsten, near Randers in Jutland, had lost eight of its hundred people, executed by the Germans. One woman lost her husband, her son, and her son-in-law, and her two daughters were given prison sentences, one for life. In Copenhagen the rioting reached new heights of violence; forty Nazi shops, including the Stella Nova and the Bulldog store in Nørrebrogade, were destroyed by fire, but there was no looting. The Germans and the Schalburg were now shooting more or less at random, and several more Danes were killed. That night the tramway officials went out on strike, because the Germans had been shooting at conductors.

By Friday, the last day of June, the strike was total. Many people had fled the city, aware that the situation would get nothing but worse, and those who could manage it were lucky to leave. The strike now included factories, offices, shops, railroads, the radio, newspapers, the post and telegraph offices, banks, cinemas, and restaurants—everything, in fact, except the water, gas, and electricity plants, and the hospital workers.

Then the Germans began to bring in troops—troops they could ill afford to spare, since the Allies were now besieging Cherbourg—and they set up roadblocks, barbed wire, and check stations. They dug trenches, and put seventy-five-millimeter guns at Town Hall Square, Kongens Nytorv, Nørrebros Runddel, and Trianglen, and they barred all roads to the city and searched everyone who tried to enter or leave. They confiscated cars and lorries, and gave the Danes their one laugh for the week when they took troops through the streets in a bus marked "Ebberødgaard," a home for mental defectives.

Best's reaction was typical. He announced that "Every Dane is responsible for this, from the King down. German honor has been trodden underfoot. The Copenhagen rabble shall taste the whip." With that he took over the water, gas, and electricity supplies, and at eleven PM on Friday the electricity in Copenhagen flickered, dimmed, and went out. An hour later the water and gas lines wheezed and expired, and we became, for all intents and purposes, a dying community. It's strange to think that you can feel alone in the middle of a city, but that's how we felt. We were ringed by Germans, and Best promised us he would "break Copenhagen so it would never rise again."

On Saturday, Copenhagen became a battlefield. The Freedom Council put up placards throughout the city, urging that the strike continue until the Schalburg Corps were removed and the curfew and other emergency orders rescinded, and at noon Lieutenant General Richter, Commander-in-Chief for Sealand, countered with red posters announcing Copenhagen's isolation from the rest of the world. He then brought in more troops, raising the total in the city to six thousand, and reinforced them with cannon, howitzers, and Mark I and Mark II tanks, while Heinkel eighty-eights flew low over the rooftops, strafing any people they saw in the streets. Best, by now known as "the bloodhound of Copenhagen," announced a twenty-four-hour curfew, with all violators to be shot, but cooler heads in Berlin prevailed, and the order was canceled. However, the German troops and the Schalburg went on a shooting, looting, and rioting spree, with the Schalburg firing into food queues and anywhere else they saw people gathered. The Danes replied by shooting and throwing things from rooftops, and luring the Germans and the Schalburg into traps and ambushes, and it became a point of pride among the younger Danes to be the last to duck when the Germans opened fire. Street barricades were everywhere, decorated with Allied flags and RAF cockades, and the smoky streets were littered with the debris of battle. I saw a young couple unbelievably pushing a baby carriage across an empty avenue; a machine gun opened up with one long burst, and they and the wreckage of their carriage lay in an untidy heap for more than an hour before they were carted away.

The Germans now redoubled their efforts to lure the underground into the open. By using the police teletype they started rumors that Finland had capitulated (Finland was on the German side), that Sweden had declared war on Germany, and that the British had landed at Esbjerg in Jutland, but none had the desired effect. They also raided all student buildings and many garages and depots, taking seventeen students hostage (whom they later released) and confiscating almost all the remaining Danish supply of gasoline and generator fuel. They did everything they could to flush out the organized Resistance, but the organized Resistance wasn't playing. They were waiting for the Allies.

The solidarity of the people was the most heartening aspect of this whole dismal period. There was a fraternal feeling that comes, unhappily, only through wars and similar catastrophes, and people shared what they had with others and endangered their own lives to help those who were worse off than they. Some went to the lakes for water, and carried it back in pails and whatever containers they could find; I saw one elderly couple lugging a washtub between them, with enough water to supply themselves and their neighbors. On that Saturday night a butcher built a bonfire in his back yard and roasted a whole carcass on it, passing out the meat on a come-one-come-all basis, and in another part of the city saboteurs raided a Nazi bakery and gave out flour as long as it lasted to all who needed it. One restaurant owner distributed fifteen hundred food parcels—the list is endless, but the spirit behind the acts was always the same. It wasn't called the People's Strike without reason.

Incidentally, although Copenhagen was the focal point of the strike, the provinces also joined in, and when the trains, ferries, dairies, and bacon factories shut down they hit the Germans where it hurt. The Germans were dependent on Danish food, and when it was denied them they realized who had the eventual upper hand.

On Sunday morning one Dr. Walter, a German economic and trade expert, flew to Copenhagen and, under orders from Berlin, snapped the rug from under Werner Best. He ordered the water, gas, and electricity restored, and he made it clear that the threat to "break Copenhagen so it would never rise again" had been idle rhetoric. In other words, the Germans were beginning to back down. That evening, Mayor Viggo Christensen of Copenhagen and the mayors of the other area municipalities issued a joint proclamation, appealing to the people to go back to work. It was broadcast over the public-address system, but its effect was dimmed when the Germans and the Schalburg fired into the crowds who were listening. The Freedom Council announced the strike would continue until all conditions had been met, and that was that.

On Monday, July 3, Best gave in. He agreed to all the Freedom's Council's demands, which I list here mainly to show the size of the victory. They were:

1. The Schalburg were to be removed from the streets.
2. The Germans were to stop firing on innocent civilians.
3. The military posts were to be removed.
4. A discussion was to be held on the future of Schalburg.
5. The curfew was to be abolished.
6. There would be no reprisals.

This agreement, coming from the man who had vowed that "the Copenhagen rabble shall taste the whip," represented what could only be called a radical change of heart. On Tuesday the Freedom Council called for a return to work the next day, and on Wednesday the People's Strike was officially over. On that day, Best was called to Hitler's headquarters in East Prussia, where he received a chewing-out that lasted three quarters of an hour. He returned to Copenhagen a pale and somewhat thoughtful man.

Isolated incidents continued throughout the week, but considering the violence that had gone on this wasn't surprising. On Wednesday the 12th, a week after the formal end of the strike, the Freedom Council called for a two-minute silence at noon, in honor of the hundred and two Danes who'd lost their lives. The appeal was circulated by handbills and broadcast over the clandestine "Hjemmefrontens Radio," and when the Town Hall clock began to strike the hour, the whole of Copenhagen stopped. Cyclists, lorries, buses, trams, pedestrians, factories—everything—and the people stood with bared heads. The only sound was faint chuffing of the engines in a few woodburning cars. Those German soldiers in evidence stood nervously at attention, not knowing what would happen next. For some reason this silence seemed more absolute than that at the annual observance on April 9; perhaps it was that the events were so much closer, and the people still felt them so deeply, that their silence was that much more meaningful. I don't know. Silent is silent, and there technically should be no gradation, but this silence was so intense it seemed to ring.

I was on the side of Town Hall Square near the *Politiken* office, and when everything started to move again I looked at my watch to see if I had time to go home before going to work. (I'd been upped from copyboy to reporter, which gave me more leeway and more time out of the office.) I badly needed some clean clothes, and it seemed to me this was as good a time as any to see what I could find. Living as I had been between two or three places, my life was somewhat disorganized. I figured I had plenty of time to get home, make what change I could, and be back at the office before the afternoon assignments were given out.

On my way up Vester Voldgade, I saw an astonishing thing. There were many people around but the street was by no means crowded, and when a lone German officer approached I gave him no more thought than to make sure he wasn't coming at me. But he seemed to have nothing particular on his mind until, right beside him, a Dane closed in, produced a pistol, and put it in his ribs. They both stopped, and while the officer looked around for help the Dane quietly reached over, slipped the officer's gun out of its holster, put it in his pocket, and walked off. The whole thing had been transacted with no more fuss than if the man had been buying a newspaper. The officer gazed about in a stunned way for a few moments and then continued walking, this time slightly faster.

I was still thinking about this as I turned into our street, remembering with delight the look on the officer's face, and I either didn't see or my mind failed to register the Volkswagen parked halfway up the block. I let myself into the house, and was in the living room when I caught the familiar rancid smell, mixed with cigar smoke. It was stronger than usual, but before I could react a man appeared through the curtains behind me, and I saw the flat, pockmarked face of Klaus Kemmerich, the Gestapo officer. He was wearing the usual belted trenchcoat, and kept his hands in the pockets. His face didn't change expression; he seemed almost bored as he nodded his head toward the door.

"Let's go," was all he said.

Chapter Fifteen

The large, black letters over the entrance to Dagmar House seemed to leer at me as I walked beneath them into the lobby. It was remarkable how the Nazis could take a drab, square office building and turn it into a personification of evil; suffice it to say that to this day I can't look at Dagmar House, even with all its neon signs (SAS, Austin, Luxor Radio Hi-Fi Stereo, American Express, Kampsax), without feeling the chill that frosted my neck as I went in with Kemmerich and his silent companion. My one faint ray of hope was that, to my knowledge, they had nothing specific on me; if they knew the truth, I was as good as dead.

The only other time I'd seen Kemmerich had been the night he stopped Ole and Sigvald and me after we'd set fire to the boot factory. I hadn't had a good look at him then because of the darkness, but now, as I stared at him across the desk in his office, which was decorated only with the usual photograph of Hitler, I saw why the Gestapo had the reputation it did. This wasn't the face of a detective, or even a policeman; it was the face of a lout who'd been given power by the system and whose strength lay only in the use of that power. I compared him with SS Officer Schlemmer, but there was really no comparison; Schlemmer was a man with training and discipline and convictions, whereas this man's training, if any, had come behind bars in some prison. Even the fact that he'd caught me indicated nothing more than dogged persistence on his part, because I'd been caught by my own stupidity and nothing else. And I told myself that if I was to survive I'd have to stop being stupid—right now.

Kemmerich had spoken bad Danish to us before, but now, in German, he asked me if I spoke his language. I did, but saw no reason for letting him know it.

"Nur ein bischen," I told him, meaning I spoke only a little.

"Then we'll get an interpreter," he said, and made a motion to the other man. This was precisely what I'd hoped, because it would give me an extra few seconds to think of my answers while the interpreter was translating.

Kemmerich produced a pack of cigarettes and offered me one, and when I shook my head he leaned back, and studied me as though I were a strange animal in the zoo. Then he reached into his desk, withdrew a folder, and began to flick through it. The room seemed suddenly to become boiling hot, and I began to perspire.

A thin, wispy man with glasses appeared, followed by a man with a notebook, and at Kemmerich's direction they both were seated. Then he looked at me, and began speaking in German.

"When did you last see your mother?" he asked.

I thought of the various times I'd seen her at Uncle Mogens', but obviously couldn't mention them. "Last October," I said.

"Where?"

"At home. Just before you arrested her."

"What makes you think we arrested her?"

I shrugged. "If a person disappears, that's what one must assume."

"What cause would we have to arrest her?"

"How would I know? What cause did you have to arrest me?"

"We'll get to that. Did you know your mother was making illegal arms with the terrorists Jørgensen?"

"That's impossible. She doesn't know one end of a gun from the other."

"That's as may be. Did you know your father was caught while illegally trying to smuggle Jewish saboteurs out of the country?"

While the translation was going on, I decided to see what I could find out about my father. "I don't know what he was doing," I said. "I just know you killed him."

"What makes you think we killed him?"

"Didn't you?"

"Answer my question. Who told you we'd killed him?"

Oops. Watch it. "Nobody told me. We'd heard nothing from him, so we assumed he was dead."

"But when you heard nothing from your mother you assumed she was arrested. What's the difference?"

Think fast. "No difference. Being arrested by you is the same as being dead."

"You think?"

"So I'm told. At any rate, my father's dead."

"He is not. He's in Vestre Prison."

"That's nice to know." It was, as a matter of fact, a relief to know he hadn't been deported.

He opened the folder in front of him. "You have something of a record yourself," he said, and I felt my mouth go dry.

He seemed to be waiting for an answer, so I said, "I

don't know what you mean. I haven't done anything."

"No?" He picked up a paper. "On Saturday, April 13, 1940, you and the ruffian Ole Suensen were caught by Standartenführer Walther Schlemmer of the Waffen-SS, while defacing the Hotel d'Angleterre with anti-German slogans. Is that correct?"

"Uh—well, more or less," I said.

"Later that same day, you and Suensen broke into the Østergade High School, where you used the school mimeograph machine for the purpose of printing inflammatory anti-German lies. Is that correct?"

"No," I said, wondering why we hadn't been picked up sooner and deciding this must be a bluff.

He looked at me over the top of the paper. "Then why were your fingerprints found on the mimeograph stencil?" he asked.

I remembered leaving the stencil behind, and wanting to go back for it but being prevented by Ole, and I swallowed. "What makes you think they were my fingerprints?" I said.

"They match those we took from your room."

"That's impossible."

He waved a hand in dismissal. "No matter. Those were just boyish pranks, compared with your later activities."

"Like what?"

He looked at me hard. "Do you know a man named Holger Andersen?"

"Yes. He was my patrol leader in the Boy Scouts."

"When did you last see him?"

Careful, now. Stick to the truth. "I don't remember exactly. I ran into him a couple of times in Tivoli."

"When?"

"I said I don't remember. Sometime last spring. May, I guess."

"Have you seen him since?"

I pretended to think. "Now that you mention it, I guess not. Why? Has he been arrested, too?"

"No."

"If you think he's a saboteur, you're wrong. I believe Holger's too clean a character to do anything like that. You know the training they give you in the Scouts—"

"I know all about it. And you last saw him in May. What did you talk about?"

"As a matter of fact, we talked about the Scouts. Just reminiscing, sort of."

He gave me a really hard stare. "Why?"

"What else do old friends talk about? I hadn't seen him for a long while."

"You just told me you ran into him a couple of times."

"Only once to talk to."

"You mean you tried to avoid him the other times?"

"No. I was busy."

"Doing what?"

"If you must know, I was late for an appointment."

"With whom?"

"A girl."

"You mean Ingrid Nielsen?"

My throat closed. My first instinct was to ask him how he knew about Ingrid, but instead I said, "No. Someone else."

He leafed through some more papers. "And you swear to me you have no idea where your mother is."

"That is correct."

He looked at the man who'd been standing silently in the door. "Bäumer, I think this man needs a refresher course," he said. Then, to me, "When your memory has improved, we'll talk again."

Bäumer took me to a small, bare room in the cellar, where he made me strip and took my clothes away. He came back with, among other things, a radio, and I see no point in going into any further details, other than to say that the radio was used to drown out the noise I made. (Radios were always playing at full volume somewhere in the building.) My memory is mercifully vague about a lot of it; I remember lights and darkness and noise and a great many different forms of pain—some sharp, some dull, some grinding, and some like bright flame—and they alternated with glorious periods of unconsciousness. I have no idea how long it lasted; it simply seemed to be a way of life.

I was interviewed by Kemmerich at intervals, and we went through the same questions and the same answers with the formalized monotony of the mating dance of the albatross, and then I would go back to my cell for another session with Bäumer. What they wanted to know, aside from my mother's whereabouts, was what had happened to Holger Andersen and who had been responsible; they were obviously more interested in Holger than in my mother, but Kemmerich used her as an alternate, to try to throw me off balance. Balance—I could barely walk during some of the later sessions.

Finally I was transferred to Shell House and a period of recuperation. There was a mixed bag of prisoners in Shell House, perhaps sixty or seventy in all, some of them hostages, some recently arrested Danes awaiting interrogation, and some like myself, whose cases were yet to be disposed of. There were even two members of the Freedom Council, although the Nazis weren't fully aware of who they were. Sometimes, if the interrogation had been routine and the prisoner apparently unimportant, he was released on the provision that he sign a paper saying he'd been well treated, and that he shave and clean himself up before leaving. Such, needless to say, was not my case; I would either become a hostage, subject to execution on German whim, or a prisoner for the rest of the war.

It was not quite a month after my arrest that eleven hostages were executed in reprisal for the liquidation of an informer. They were brought from Vestre to Shell House, where they were lined up and shot, one by one, in the back of the neck. We could hear the shots, and in short order the grapevine brought word of what had happened, and for a terrible few hours I thought my father might have been one of them. But he wasn't, and I felt the small relief of knowing there was still a bit of hope for all of us. Just what it was, I couldn't have said.

The grapevine was an interesting thing. Here we were, supposedly sealed off from the rest of the world, yet within a short time of something's happening we knew about it, not always in full detail but with reasonable accuracy. Thus we knew, on August 15, that the Freedom Council called a twenty-four-hour strike to protest the shooting of the hostages, and the Germans did nothing to interfere with it. Except for the public utilities, nothing moved for twenty-four hours, and there were similar strikes throughout the country during that week. Finally General Pancke lost his temper. Declaring that "those eleven in the Shell House were evidently not enough," he ordered a hundred and ninety prisoners deported to Germany as hostages, and when news of this got out the strikes started again. This time, however, the Germans weren't passive about it; on the morning of Saturday, September 16, a squad car with fifteen soldiers drove into Town Hall Square and machine-gunned the people waiting for the morning papers. Twenty-three were wounded, and several later died.

Then, on Tuesday the 19th, the Germans rang the air-raid alarms, and when the Danish police went to their emergency stations the Germans attacked and attempted to disarm them. But the police fought back, and there were skirmishes and pitched battles all around the city. The guard at Amalienborg fought particularly hard, and they, aided by civilians who swarmed in to help, managed to keep the Germans away from the palace. In all, two thousand of the nine-thousand-man police force were arrested and sent to German concentration camps; the remainder went underground. The police force ceased to exist, and the Danes took to maintaining order among themselves. A private watch corps was set up, under the direction of the Freedom Council, and thieves were either thrashed on the spot or locked in cellars—sometimes both. Everything considered, the system worked fairly well.

Deprived of the Schalburg Corps, the Germans organized a similar outfit known as the *Hilfspolizei,* shortened to *Hipos,* or "police helpers," who wore black uniforms, had sidearms and police dogs, and were composed of those Danish Nazis who had nowhere else to go and had to stake everything on the fading hope of a German victory. The desperate nature of their existence made them mean as tarantulas. A German-organized, armed anti-sabotage group called the Sommer Corps was designed to replace the Danish factory guards, whose hearts had never really been in it, but by this time the sabotage was so widespread that no amount of prevention could stop it. Things were cranking toward the finale, but with the certainty of an Allied victory the Nazi savagery increased. Once you could feel safe if there was no concrete proof against you; now nobody was safe, because the Germans were determined to take everybody down with them when they went. It was a far cry from the old days of "Wir werden uns systematisch beliebt machen."

My cellmate was a wiry little telegrapher whom I knew only as Oni, who'd been captured a week before and who was still being interrogated. They hadn't yet got around to torturing him; his sessions were reasonably civilized, and each time he returned to our room he brought with him more information than he'd gone out with. I never found how he did it, but it seemed as though he had a wireless antenna in his head; he'd be gone for two or three hours, and come back bursting with news. The last day of October he had a particularly long session, and when he returned he was grinning so broadly I could count his missing teeth.

"Man, did we clobber them!" he said, sitting down and stretching his legs.

"Who?" I asked.

"The Gestapo, at Aarhus." (Gestapo headquarters in Jutland were housed in the University of Aarhus.)

"How'd we do it?"

"Well, the RAF were the ones who did it. We fed them the dope, and they sent in a flight of Mosquitoes that just plastered the place. At least two hundred Gestapo killed." He rubbed his hands together.

I looked out the window. "I wonder what would happen if they sent Mosquitoes here," I said. (De Havilland Mosquitoes were fast, low-level bombers made out of plywood, which gave a poor radar echo and was therefore hard to detect. The planes had two engines, and were so small the bombardier had to lie flat on his stomach.)

"It'd probably be the same thing," Oni replied. "Those things are here and gone before you know it."

"Yes, but we're on the top floor," I said. "It would be we who got plastered, not the Gestapo."

Oni shrugged. "Win a few, lose a few. You can't have everything."

He reminded me a little of Ole, and I wondered how he'd survived as long as he had. "What else do you know?" I asked.

"Nothing much. The Krauts are putting hostages on all their troop trains in Jutland. Every last one. Fat lot of good it does them, though; we just time the fuses to go off after the third or fourth car, and the hostage isn't hurt."

"Where'd you get this?"

He grinned. "A little bird told me."

It's a strange thing about being in jail; after a while you lose all sense of time, and you become numb to everything except the minutiae of everyday existence. Small things, that you hardly ever thought about before, now seem important, such as hot food and a clean place to sleep, and a place where you can stretch your legs and walk about a bit. The larger things appear to fade away and become part of another world. In a way this is good, because otherwise the monotony could very easily drive you crazy. Even danger can become monotonous, if drawn out over a long period of time.

The main news that winter was the continued advance of the Allied armies once the Battle of the Bulge was over. That had been the Germans' final effort to split the invading forces, and after that it was simply a matter of time. In Denmark, however, the pace of the fighting increased, with bombings and counter-bombings taking place daily, and executions and counter-executions happening at the same rate. The RAF was literally pouring arms and explosives in to the Resistance fighters, and they were putting it all to good use. Probably the most spectacular event of the winter was on January 5, when the Tuborg Breweries were wrecked by the Brøndum gang, but it was just one on the long list of senseless bombings. John Steinbeck wrote later that the Germans, in their retreat, "ran through Europe like cruel children," destroying whatever they could get their hands on, and it's as good a description as any for what happened in Denmark.

One day—I didn't know the date at the time, but I found

out later it was March 21—Oni looked out the window and, after studying the sky for a while, said, "I have a feeling something's going to happen today."

"What?" I asked. "How do you know?"

"It's about time, that's all."

"Time for *what*?" After months of sharing the same room I was becoming edgy, and impatient with Oni's omniscience.

"I don't know. I may be wrong." He went to the door and looked speculatively at the lock, and I flung myself on my cot and faced the wall. Somewhere a radio was playing at full volume, and I wondered what poor blighter was getting the treatment. I tried to close my ears, but the music seeped through; it was "Beer Barrel Polka," known to the Germans as "Rosamunde," and it was like all the German bands in hell.

Then I heard another sound. It was a low growl, which grew quickly to a roar, then came the hammering of machine-gun fire, and then the air exploded all around us. Oni was standing at the window, screaming with laughter and pointing, and as the building jolted and shook under the bomb blasts I joined him, and saw airplanes flashing past so close I could see the pale faces of the pilots in their cockpits. They were Mosquitoes, and they came over in waves, bombing and strafing the building. Then the smoke got too heavy for us to see more, and we turned our attention to breaking down the door. We were on the top floor, five stories up, and unless we wanted to burn to death we had to get out of there fast. But the door wouldn't budge. We shook it and punched it and threw ourselves against it, and we shouted for help as loud as we could, but the only answer was the crash of bombs and the smoke beginning to curl up through the building. Then, miraculously, a figure appeared; it was Danish Police Captain Lyst

Hansen, one of the prisoners, and he had a bundle of keys in his hand and was unlocking the cell doors.

"Hansen!" Oni shouted, as the Captain fumbled with our lock. "Where'd you get the keys?"

"I talked a guard into giving them to me," Hansen replied. Our door swung open. "Now get out of here," he said, unnecessarily. "If you don't hurry, you'll have to jump."

Finding our way out through the smoke and flames was something else again. People were running around and shouting and crying, and it became a race for the ground floor, which turned out to be more heavily damaged than the top. (It developed later that the RAF, knowing the Gestapo records were on the lower floors, had dropped delayed-action bombs, which went off at the ground level and completely wrecked the files. One, in fact, dropped into the courtyard in the center of the building, and when it exploded wiped out everything in the surrounding area.)

How we got out I honestly don't know. The confusion was such that nobody gave any thought to our being escaping prisoners; it was every man for himself, and get to the fresh air as fast as you can. The rule in a burning building is to keep close to the floor, where the air is better, and put your jacket over your nose and mouth to filter out the smoke, but when you're on the upper floors you're in trouble no matter what you do. Oni and I clawed our way down through the choking blackness, our only illumination the orange flames, and at last, when my lungs felt as though I'd inhaled a blowtorch, we staggered out onto the street. The confusion there was total, and we used the last of our strength running two blocks away before we collapsed.

The results of that raid were mixed. The records and the building were destroyed, a lot of Gestapo and collaborators were killed, and a number of hostages (including the two

Freedom Council men) escaped, so that was all to the good. But eight of the hostages lost their lives and, what was most hideous, one of the first Mosquitoes hit the flagpole atop the railroad station and crashed into a nearby Catholic school; its smoke was mistaken for bomb damage by another flight, and it unloaded its bombs on the school, killing eighty-eight children and twenty-four nuns and other adults. It may be true, as Oni said, that you win a few and you lose a few, but that kind of losing does a lot to spoil the taste of the winning.

Chapter Sixteen

In a dimly lighted passage to the dungeons under Kronborg Castle, in Elsinore, sits the brooding statue of Holger Danske—the Holger the Dane of Hans Christian Andersen's story—armed and resting on his shield. It's said that whenever the country is in peril he leaves the castle and walks abroad at night, and if this is so he must have done a great deal of walking that last winter of the war. There were those who claimed to have seen him, and I would be the last one to doubt their word.

When I escaped from Shell House, after eight months' confinement, it was like going from a prison into a madhouse. The whole German machine was coming apart at the seams; the organization and the discipline were dissolving, and the bombings and murders were wholly without pattern. There had once been a sort of Teutonic neatness about the murders, in that they would shoot a dozen or so Danes on the very spot where one of their men or collaborators had been killed, but now they just fired at random. The Danes, naturally, retaliated, and this did nothing to make the Germans any more loving.

One further complication was that, as the Allied armies drove into Germany, German refugees came streaming into Denmark; they were frightened and disorganized but they were also arrogant, and loud in their demands for food and lodging. They elbowed their way around, expecting the Danes as an occupied nation to accommodate them, and they were furious when they didn't receive the polite obeisance they expected. To many, it came as a shock that the Danes weren't the happy cousins they'd been told about, and that the Model Protectorate wasn't so model after all. When a dream as grandiose as the Nazis' starts dissolving into reality, the shock is proportionately jarring.

My first thought, after Oni and I parted, was to get to Uncle Mogens' and find out about my mother. The fact that they'd stopped questioning me about her made me fear they might have arrested her, but I tried to convince myself they'd have told me if they had, simply as another form of torture. My next thought, which followed hard on the heels of the first, was that I was now an escaped prisoner, subject to arrest on sight, and I'd have to be extremely careful where I went and whom I saw. When you go underground you must be doubly suspicious of everyone, and you shouldn't sleep more than one night in the same place. The safest thing, naturally, would be to take the course of many other fugitives and go to Sweden, but I felt that would somehow be quitting. There was too much keeping me in Denmark to sit out the rest of the war in safety.

Don't ask me why, but as I approached Uncle Mogens' house I knew she wasn't there. The house looked the same as it always had, but there was something about it that said "empty," and when I knocked on the door there was no answer. I waited, and gave the knock again, then decided I shouldn't be seen waiting around like that. If there'd been a raid, or an arrest, or whatever (I wouldn't allow myself to think of a murder), informers might be watching to see who else came to the house, and it was no place for me. I walked quickly away, trying to quiet the fear that made my heart feel like lead.

My next move was to get hold of Stig, and find out what had happened. I went to the dental clinic but it was closed and in desperation I went to Sigvald's house. I gave the ritual knock, and after a few moments the door opened a crack and Sigvald's wife peered out. Then she opened the door wider, said, "Come in," and closed it fast behind me. "Get down in the cellar," she said, pointing to a door off the kitchen.

I opened the door and found I'd walked into a broom closet so I backed out and said, "Excuse me. Which is the cellar door?"

With an expression as though she were teaching a child to spell, she took a screwdriver from a tool rack in the closet, laid the metal part of it across two brass coat hooks, and there was a click and the back of the closet swung open, revealing a flight of stairs. "I forgot you hadn't been around lately," she said, replacing the screwdriver in its rack. "We've gone modern."

I smelled the cool dampness of the cellar and the fumes from an oil lamp, and when I reached the foot of the stairs I saw Stig and Sigvald sitting at a table. There was a mass of drawings and diagrams between them, and around the perimeter of the cellar, faintly illuminated by the flickering lamplight, were workbenches, drill presses, and assorted tools. Stig's glasses gleamed as he stood up to greet me.

"Well, stone the crows!" he exclaimed, holding out his hand. "We thought they had you for the duration!"

"They would have, but for the RAF," I replied. "Do you know where my mother is?"

There was a brief pause, just enough for my heart to do a flip, and Stig said, "No, not exactly."

"Is she all right?"

"Oh, yes. She's fine."

"What about Uncle Mogens?"

Stig cleared his throat. "He's dead."

"An informer?" I asked, feeling sick.

"We don't know. They just went into his shop, and shot him to pieces."

"Somebody must have informed."

He shrugged. "Or was followed."

"And my mother?"

"She was out at the time. She came back after they'd left."

"And you don't know where she is now?"

"No. But she comes here every now and then."

"Will you give her a message?"

"Of course."

"Just tell her I'm all right, and I'll try to see her as soon as I can."

"Where are you staying?"

"I don't know. I've got to keep moving."

"Maybe we can help with that. We know several people who'll take in—ah—transients."

"That would be good. I'll need all the help I can get." I looked at the plans on the table, and said, "What are you doing—building a bridge?"

"No, blowing one," Sigvald replied. "You recognize it?"

I looked more closely, and saw it was the Langebro, connecting Copenhagen with the island of Amager, over which Ole and I had ridden on our first foray to get explosives. It's a big bridge, with trolley tracks in the middle of the roadway, and it looked like a job for the RAF instead of saboteurs. "How do you plan to do it?" I asked.

He looked at me with quiet sarcasm. "We're going to kick it down," he said.

"May I help?"

"I think you'd better lie low for a while," Stig said. "We don't want you caught again, and besides, you may need a refresher course, to bring you up to date."

I thought of Bäumer's so-called refresher course, and it seemed to have happened in another world and another century. "I'll do whatever you say," I replied. Then, with the prospect of a certain amount of inaction ahead, my thoughts went to Ingrid. "Do you think I could get a message to someone?" I asked.

"Who?" said Stig.

"A young lady."

"Is she reliable?"

"Yes." I thought briefly of her father, but decided he was no problem.

"We can get a messenger for you. What would you like to say?"

I cleared my throat. "Just that I'd like to see her."

The upshot was that they found me a series of places to sleep—student rooms, attics, basements, stores, and in some cases even bedrooms—and I rotated among them, never sleeping in the same place twice in succession. They got me a forged ration card so I could eat, and I managed to do enough for the paper to have money to live on. It was a precarious existence, but I was able to get by.

A twelve-year-old boy took my message to Ingrid. His parents had been shot by the Germans and he was passionately dedicated to working for the Resistance; his only complaint was that they never gave him anything to do except carry messages, and he was hoping the war would last long enough for him to graduate to sabotage or executions. When I told him the message he looked at me with scorn, and vanished. I was staying that night in a vacant room in the back of a candy store; there had been no candy in the place for several years, but the memory of it lingered in the walls, and the air smelled sweet and faintly cloying. Even the bed in the back room smelled of candy, and I theorized the owner had probably taken a bag of chocolate caramels to bed with him every night. For someone as undernourished as I, the smell was maddening.

She came in through the back door, and for a moment we just looked at each other. Then we were embracing. I don't think anyone spoke a complete sentence for ten minutes, and when, finally, I was able to put the words together I said, "Welcome to the candy store."

"Welcome indeed," said Ingrid, and again the conversation ended.

The first thing you say at the end of a long silence is not likely to be very important, or even intelligent, and my case was no exception. I looked at the ceiling, cleared my throat, and said, "How's your father?"

Ingrid laughed. "He's all right. Why?"

"I just wondered."

"Do I remind you of him?"

"Not a great deal."

"That's a relief."

I hadn't planned it this way, but I suddenly saw an opening, and decided to try it. "I was wondering how he'd react to being my father-in-law," I said.

Ingrid turned and looked at me, and her eyes suddenly and unaccountably filled with tears. "He'd better love it," she said, and that was that. It just goes to show how you can occasionally get married as a result of talking about something else. It's a tricky business all around.

And, as a parenthetical observation, being underground had its drawbacks, but it also had the advantage that you weren't hampered by parents while courting. The seclusion on which your life depended worked to your advantage in a number of ways.

They blew up the Langebro on March 27, and I was sorry not to have had a hand in it. It was the most ambitious and possibly the single most successful sabotage action of the war, because there were several coal barges and ships laden with goods for Germany that were bottled up in Copenhagen harbor as a result, and their badly needed cargoes were never delivered. The railroad sabotage had virtually strangled the overland transportation of materials to Germany, and this more or less put the lid on the whole thing. I heard that Sigvald missed the explosion because of a complicated delivery at the hospital, but his hand in the planning was far more valuable than his presence at the actual detonation. He said later he felt like da Vinci not being allowed to see the finished *Mona Lisa*.

The two minutes' silence on April 9 was a particularly meaningful one, because everyone felt it would be the last such observance—at least the last during wartime. Town Hall Square was crowded, as usual, and the silence was total for only a few seconds before there was the sound of shooting. Everyone looked around to see where it came from, and then came the crack of more shots, and people began to run for the newly completed bomb shelters. It developed that Germans and Hipos were shooting into the crowd in an attempt to start a riot, which would give them an excuse to do some real killing. It disrupted the silence, but it didn't gain them anything more than that. You have to say for those people that they didn't give up easily—although of course the Hipos had nothing to lose.

It was the middle of April when we knew the end was near. The Allies were crowding into Germany from all sides, and had just started to discover the real horror of the Nazi death camps. Suddenly, nobody in Germany knew anything about it; it seemed that nobody had even belonged to the Nazi party. They were all well-meaning people who'd been deceived. In this general atmosphere, Count Folke Bernadotte of the Swedish Red Cross had been able to arrange with Heinrich Himmler to have the Danish Jews and policemen released from the camps and taken by bus to Sweden, a trip that naturally went through their homeland. They were released on April 15, a Sunday (after promising to tell all who asked that their sojourn had been "productive and happy"), and as the caravan of Swedish buses, with red crosses on their roofs and sides, approached Denmark's southern border the word spread ahead of them. At every village people jammed the roadside, waving Danish flags and shouting *"Velkommen til Danmark!* Welcome to Denmark!" and when they reached Copenhagen the crowd was several hundred thousand strong. The buses came down Vesterbrogade from Roskilde, passed the railroad station, then crossed Town Hall Square on their way to the docks for the ferry to Malmø, their destination in Sweden, and the cheering and rejoicing were so loud that the Germans finally announced, over their public-address loud-speakers, that unless demonstration quieted down the prisoners would be returned to Germany. The people stopped throwing flowers and stopped cheering, but they continued to wave their flags and beam their joy, and the buses went to the docks through a silent sea of grinning, flag-waving Danes. Needless to say the prisoners were smiling too—although most were also weeping—and the only glum faces were those of the Gestapo guards on the buses, who somehow took the whole thing as a personal insult.

One thing everyone remarked on was how well the Danish Jews looked, and it turned out that they, almost alone among the inmates of German concentration camps, had fared reasonably well because they'd been allowed to receive food packages from home, and their fellow Danes had seen to it they were well supplied. In fact, only fifty-two had died in the camp, which considering their average age was about the rate to be expected. The prisoners were unlucky in some things, but they were lucky in being Danes. The policemen's condition was not so good.

I had watched them as they crossed Town Hall Square, and was affected to the point where my throat hurt and my vision began to blur. I felt suddenly homesick, and when the buses had gone I turned and headed for our house, knowing it was foolish but convinced if I was careful I wouldn't be caught. I don't know why I did it; it was a homing instinct of some sort, and I gave in to it. Just be careful, I told myself. You were caught before because you were careless, and now you've learned that lesson. Just be careful.

At the top of our street I stopped, close to the building line, and surveyed the scene. The street was absolutely empty —not a car, not a person, not a dog was in sight. Near the far end was a pile of rubbish and empty cartons, debris from either a hurried moving or a raid of some sort, and on the sidewalk a few yards from where I stood was a bunch of withered flowers, brown and crisp and faded, marking the spot where some luckless Dane had been shot. I looked at the windows of the houses to see if anyone was watching, but they stared back at me like so many blind eyes, and I began to feel I'd come to a section of the city from which everyone had fled. Then, when I'd checked everything else, I looked at our house, and was astonished to see that two of the windows were open, their curtains moving gently in the breeze. I ducked back around the corner and then, flat against the building, put my head out just far enough to see our house. I couldn't tell if anyone was inside; all I could see were the open windows and the white curtains, and for fully ten minutes I stood there motionless, waiting. Then two bare arms appeared and pulled one of the windows closed, and in a moment did the same with the other window, and I was able to see enough of the face to know it was my mother. I shouted, raced across the street, flung open the door, and burst into the house.

It was the same as our meeting at Uncle Mogens', except this time she wept more, and clung to me as though I were trying to get away. When, finally, she was coherent, she said, "I thought you were dead. I thought they'd shot you." And then she began to weep again.

"Didn't Stig tell you?" I said. "I asked him to give you a message."

"I haven't seen him," she replied. "I've been working in Odense."

"You shouldn't be here now," I told her. "This is where they caught me. It's dangerous."

"Then what are you doing here?" She released me, reached in the pocket of her dress for a grubby handkerchief, and blew her nose.

"I just came to check," I said. "Neither of us should be here."

She balled the handkerchief into a little wad, and wiped her eyes. "When they got you, I didn't care what happened," she said. "I figured that with you and your father gone I had nothing to live for, so I'd live dangerously and do as much as I could before they got me. It's so long since I've been careful I've forgotten what it's like." She sniffed, and laughed. "Now I guess I'll have to start all over again."

"Papa's all right," I said. "Last time I heard, he was in Vestre." I didn't mention that he might have been one of the hundred and ninety General Pancke deported to Germany; I saw no point in bringing it up.

"Then I'll have to be doubly careful," she said. "And I've still got so much to do."

"Like what?" I had no idea what she was doing for the

Resistance, but it was clearly more than just grenade pins.

"For one thing, I've got to clean up the Jakobys' house," she said. "It hasn't been touched in a year and a half."

"What are you talking about?"

"We're all doing it. We're fixing up the homes of those who were taken prisoner, so when they come back it'll look pretty. I'm going to have fresh flowers for the Jakobys as soon as I know when they're coming."

"There's still a war on. They're not going to be coming back right away."

"It won't be long. And there's a lot to be done."

"I'll tell you one thing—it doesn't take them long to catch you. When the Gestapo moves, they move fast."

She shook her head. "I'm not worried about them any more. They've got too many big problems to waste time on the likes of me." She hesitated, looking for the right word, then said, "Jens, do you mind if I ask you something?"

"Of course not. What would you like to know?"

"How long is it since you've had a bath?"

I knew I was home.

My mother was right. In those last two weeks the German deterioration was so fast and so complete that the Gestapo gave up any pretense of police work, and simply joined in the general, random murdering. It was safer to be in your home than on the streets, because you never knew when a German or a Hipo would start shooting. I stayed in most of the time, and helped my mother put the house back in shape, and in the evenings we listened to the BBC and followed the progress of the war. Thus on May 1 we heard of Hitler's death, and on May 2 of the fall of Berlin to the Russians, and on May 4, in the middle of the news, the announcer stopped, paused, and said, "We have a special bulletin. Field Marshal Montgomery has just announced that the German troops in Holland, northwest Germany, and Denmark have capitulated."

My mother and I looked at each other, and then she burst into tears and we embraced. We heard faint noises outside, which became louder and resolved into shouting and cheering, and she went to the window and pulled aside the blackout curtain. All down the street, and then throughout the city, lights were appearing; people had taken off their blackout curtains and put candles in their windows, and Copenhagen began to glow as though lighted by millions of fireflies. My mother ripped off the curtain and put a candle in the window, and we did the same with all the other windows, and as we did we saw that bonfires were beginning to appear in the streets, where people were burning their blackout curtains. We joined them, and threw our curtains on the fire, and with each new blaze the cheering grew louder, until you couldn't even hear yourself shout. Flags appeared—British, American, Russian, and Danish flags—and people began to go wildly insane. They danced, they hugged, they kissed, and they cried; in all my life, I hadn't kissed as many strangers as I did that night, except that nobody was a stranger because we were all one. When, physically exhausted and drained of emotion, we went home, my mother put new candles in the windows, and as she lighted the last one she said, "This one's for your father. It'll stay here until he returns."

At four twenty-five the next afternoon British troops arrived at Kastrup, flown in by American Dakota transports, and there was sporadic, savage fighting as the roundup of the Hipos and collaborators began. In all, four hundred people were killed or wounded in Copenhagen before all the traitors were caught, and it was a long time before everything was straightened out. But May 5 was technically Liberation Day, and is remembered as such. It was summed up best by a sign hung that day in a small store, which read: "Closed because of great joy."

My father came home the next day. We heard his footsteps on the stairs and my mother ran to meet him, and I decided to hold back and let her have him first. Knowing his liking for understated humor I thought it might be a good joke if I pretended he'd never been gone, and I was trying out different phrases in my mind when he came into the room, my red-eyed mother clinging to his arm. He was thin and pale, and he looked at me with faint surprise.

"Why, Jens," he said. "Why aren't you in school?"

Format by Gloria Bressler
Set in 11 pt. Old Style #1
Composed, printed and bound by The Haddon Craftsmen, Inc.
Scranton, Pa.
HARPER & ROW, PUBLISHERS, INCORPORATED